101

POSITIVE STEPS
TOWARD EMPLOYMENT
WITH AUTISM

SOCIAL SKILLS FOR THE WORKPLACE

Lisa Tew, MS, CCC-SLP   co-author of *Autism and Employment*

Positive Steps Toward Employment with Autism

Social Skills for the Workplace

All marketing and publishing rights guaranteed to and reserved by:

FUTURE HORIZONS INC.

721 W. Abram Street

Arlington, TX 76013

(800) 489-0727

(817) 277-0727

(817) 277-2270 (fax)

E-mail: info@fhautism.com

www.fhautism.com

ISBN: 9781941765159

To my mother, Jean Elizabeth Havens, whose generous spirit embraces diversity in nature and in people.

Contents

Lisa Tew and I are colleagues, friends, and of the same mind when it comes to the most important learning that must take place for individuals on the autism spectrum: the soft skills that are so valued by employers and that are crucial to successful relationships, meaningful employment, and independence. Working together in the schools, we see many students on the autism spectrum with strong cognitive and academic abilities who struggle to learn soft skills, particularly social-communication skills. The consequence is that, despite having a strong knowledge base and technical skills, they are likely to be unemployed or underemployed as adults, and indeed research has shown us that employment engagement and success for individuals on the autism spectrum is extremely low.

Lisa and I were frustrated by the academic focus and time limitations present in the schools and inspired by the capable young people we knew on the autism spectrum and their supportive families, so we wrote a book for parents and began conducting social-communication groups for those young people who were seeking employment but struggling with the social-communication skills needed to be successful. We have worked to include parents in our lessons, knowing from experience that parents are naturally deeply invested in their children's success and have the most teachable moments and the most opportunities to guide new skill development and create meaningful change.

In our book, *Autism and Employment: Raising Your Child with Foundational Skills for the Future*, we researched those soft skills that are the foundation to successful employment and matched them with what we called "foundational" social-communication skills. This book was primarily written for parents of older children and adolescents on the autism spectrum, to give them guidance for building their children's skills in their everyday lives in preparation for eventual transition to adulthood. In *101 Positive Steps Toward Employment With Autism: Social Skills For The Workplace*, Lisa created 101 "steps," or focused insights with practice, for responding positively to challenges in the workplace across five areas that are liable to be difficult for many young adults on the autism spectrum (making mistakes; "when things go wrong"; choosing words to say to others; communicating with body, face and voice tone; and "intensity" issues). The 101 steps incorporate themes of tolerance, advocacy, respect, reputation, and especially "positivity." The book is written for the young adult who is on the autism spectrum, but parents, job coaches, vocational counselors, and others who are providing support to a young person on the spectrum should find it very helpful for guiding positive practice and change.

Lisa has over thirty-five years of experience working with hundreds of individuals on the autism spectrum and their parents, and this book represents her insights and experience. She is a firm believer in positivity and chose to frame the 101 steps around this concept, knowing that employers are looking for employees who will be above all else "positive" in the workplace and that positive behaviors are associated with successful employment. She understands that individuals with autism quite often approach new or challenging situations with heightened anxiety which can translate into negativity, and that speaking of behaviors in terms of "positive" choices is often more helpful rather than characterizing behaviors as "right" or "wrong."

Lisa and I have gone on to create Independent Futures With Autism and our website, IFAutism.com, with the firm belief that 1) social communication skills are the foundation to successful, independent futures, 2) these skills can be developed, 3) bright young people on the autism spectrum should have bright futures, 4) parents are the best coaches long-term for their children, and 5) social communication behaviors can be positive despite the challenges. I hope you will read and share Lisa's book with young people on the autism spectrum and their parents and support people, and visit IFAutism.com to communicate with us and to read Lisa's blogs and Q&A on a variety of topics. It has been our shared mission to fill a void in supports for youth with autism who are transitioning into adulthood, and we wish you the best of luck on your journey.

– Diane Zajac, LMSW

POSITIVITY CHALLENGES AND EMPLOYMENT

Employers are looking for employees who are *positive*. Employers may list specific "hard" or technical skills that they want an employee to have for a particular job, but surveys show that employers most want to hire people who have positive "soft skills." Employers want to hire someone who can work in harmony with others, someone who can communicate and respond socially to customers, coworkers, and supervisors with positivity.

Even if you do not have experience or strong technical skills, an employer will be more interested in hiring you if you are positive. Employers may hire a person who shows positivity and then train that employee for a specific job, even if that person initially lacks the technical skills or experience for the job. Likewise, it is not enough to have technical skills or experience to get and keep a job! You need to be able to interact and communicate with others in a positive way in the workplace.

The most important thing you can do to achieve independence as a young adult is to get and maintain employment. We know that being positive is crucial to doing this. But it is often difficult to be positive: it is hard to know what positivity looks like and sounds like, when and how to do it, and what the barriers are to being positive. There are in fact many challenges to being positive, every day, for everyone. But there are certain kinds of challenges that are especially common for individuals who are on the autism spectrum. In this book you will find 101 positive steps toward employment and independence, with insights and positivity practice across five areas that you may find especially difficult. Those positivity challenge areas are:

A. When you make mistakes or think you might make mistakes

B. When things go wrong for you

C. When you are choosing words to say to others

D. When you need to communicate with your body and face and voice tone

E. When you feel very strongly about the things you like and don't like, and you have to do something that you don't like

Are any of these areas challenging or difficult for *you*? In helping you to evaluate which areas you may need more insights and practice in, I suggest that you ask people who know you well, such as your parents or other family members, also perhaps your job coach and/or vocational counselor who may have worked with you in an employment setting. Please be honest, accept that you may need to develop awareness and practice in one or more of these five areas, and don't be hard on yourself! Remember that these areas are frequently challenging for many people to stay positive in and do or say the right thing! Being aware and getting some practice will help you to make positive changes that can help you to get and keep a job. Please consider the following questions to help you determine in which areas you may need help:

A. Mistakes/Weaknesses and Positivity

Are you someone who:

- Frequently gets angry, frustrated, or anxious if you do not do well at something (e.g., you get a bad grade, lose a game, struggle to understand something, have friendship issues, or have communication issues)?

- Avoids or refuses new activities or responsibilities because you think they might be too hard, and you might fail or not be good at them?

- Feels angry when you receive criticism, corrections, or negative feedback?

- Becomes upset if you are asked to do something over or to do it in a different way?

- Gets "stuck" thinking about what you feel is a lack of success in some area?

B. Things That Go Wrong and Positivity

Are you someone who frequently gets angry, frustrated, or anxious when things go wrong or unexpected/unwanted events occur that:

- Are accidents, i.e., not done by others on purpose to hurt or bother you?

- Are things that "just happen" in life due to circumstances or chance (again, not on purpose to hurt or bother you)?

- Happen because people aren't perfect and they make mistakes or disappoint you?

C. Word Choices and Positivity

Are you someone who struggles to find and use words with others that:

- Are polite?
- Are complimentary?
- Are encouraging to others?
- Show acceptance of others?
- Show self-acceptance or positive self-concept?
- Solve problems with others?
- Are kind?
- Are tactful?
- Acknowledge and respond to others?
- Are framed or structured in a way that shows respect?
- Are on an appropriate topic for the workplace?

- Are an appropriate length/amount of talking?

- Happen at the right time and place, to the right person?

- Have positive voice tone and body language to match and support the words?

- Are "nice and necessary?"

- Share personal/sensitive information privately?

- Shift in style from casual to formal as appropriate?

D. Body Language/Voice and Positivity: Body Posture/Orientation, Facial Expression, Voice Tone and Volume

Do you struggle with:

- Showing interest in others?

- Showing respect for others?

- Looking friendly?

- Sounding friendly, respectful, and interested in others?

- Invading the personal space of others?

- Understanding the body language of others?

E. Intensity and Positivity: Strong Feelings, Preferences, and Opinions

Do you frequently:

- Get angry/frustrated when you can't do your desired or preferred activities?

- Avoid or refuse new activities, or learning or participating in new things because they are not your favorite things to do?

- Have strong opinions about topics and/or individuals?

- Have difficulty understanding and expressing what you are feeling?

- Have trouble recognizing how intense your feelings are and coping with them?

- Struggle to understand how other people may feel differently?

- Have trouble with the body language and voice tone/volume surrounding intensity?

- Need to "scale back" or limit your positive or negative intensity?

- Misinterpret situations leading to more intensity?

- Find you have no "middle ground" or back-up choices beyond your strong preference?

Any or all of these areas might be weaknesses for you and can make it hard for you to have the positivity that employers want. Why is positivity so important on the job? How can problems being positive in each of these areas become problems at work? Consider the following issues that could come up in the workplace, in each of the positivity challenge areas:

A. Mistakes/Weaknesses and Positivity

Suppose your boss asks you to do something that you don't think you can do very well, or your boss corrects you because you did something wrong. Maybe you are asked to do something new and you don't feel confident that you can do it. Perhaps you made a mistake and you don't want to try it again because you think you might do it wrong?

B. Things That Go Wrong and Positivity

Suppose you did not get the job you wanted. Maybe you didn't finish your job and you have to stay late to get it done. Perhaps someone borrows then loses a tool you needed to do your job. What if you missed a step in your job task list and you have to start over again?

C. Word Choices and Positivity

Suppose you need to tell someone to stop talking so you can do your work, but you don't want to hurt their feelings. Perhaps you want a co-worker to like you. What if you want to tell someone else how they should do something in a better way without offending them? What if you need to report a problem to your boss?

D. Body Language/Voice and Positivity

Suppose your coworkers greet you when you show up, and you need to greet them back. Suppose someone is telling you a story and you should look interested. What if you need to ask for a day off and you want your boss to agree? Perhaps you have to tell someone how to do something, but you don't want to sound bossy. Suppose your boss gives you instructions on how to do your job and you need to show him you are interested in doing the job.

E. Intensity and Positivity

Suppose you really like your current job, and your boss tells you that you need to learn to do another job in the store. What if you love to play video games all day, and having a job means you can't play video games as much as you usually do? Suppose you hate getting up early, but your job requires you to get up early. Maybe you like some things about your job, but intensely dislike other things. What if you have to work with someone you really don't like?

The following pages outline 101 positive steps toward employment and independence across the five areas above. You may want to focus on an area where you feel you need extra practice and insights, or you may work through multiple or all the areas to maximize your positivity for employment success. Whichever area(s) you choose to work on, please also do step 101, which relates to all five areas. Good luck on your journey, and stay positive!

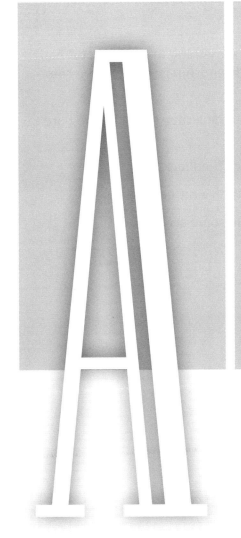

MISTAKES/WEAKNESSES AND POSITIVITY

A

Everyone makes mistakes and has areas that they can improve on! When something is hard to do, and when you make mistakes, you need to be aware of it and practice in those areas so you can improve. It is positive to learn about yourself, accept mistakes and improve weaknesses, and become comfortable doing things you thought you could not do. Suppose your boss asks you to do something that you don't think you can do very well, or your boss corrects you because you did something wrong. With practice, you can make positive choices to handle these and other challenges. This section has twenty ways to practice positive steps toward independence and employment, if you:

- Frequently get angry or frustrated if you do not do well at something (e.g., you get a bad grade, lose a game, struggle to understand something, have friendship issues, or have communication issues).

- Avoid or refuse new activities or responsibilities because you think they might be too hard, and you might fail or not be good at them.

- Feel angry when you receive criticism, corrections, or negative feedback.

- Become upset if you are asked to do something over or to do it in a different way.

- Get "stuck" thinking about what you feel is a lack of success in some area.

*It is **positive** to know your strengths.* Everyone has strengths (things they are good at), and they are different for everyone. Strengths can be "hard skills" such as driving, math, or being good at video games. The most important strengths for getting and keeping a job are "soft" skills. Look at the list of soft skills, and check the boxes for all the soft skill strengths that you have.

Soft Skills

☐ Kind

☐ Helpful

☐ Honest

☐ Friendly

☐ Upbeat

☐ Caring

☐ Thoughtful

☐ Patient

☐ Respectful

☐ Sharing

☐ Hardworking

☐ Cooperative

☐ Responsible

☐ Organized

☐ Good communicator

☐ Good self-control

It is **positive** to know your weaknesses so you can improve in those areas. Everyone has weaknesses, and they are different for everyone. The most important areas to improve for employment are soft skills. Look at the list of soft skills, and check the boxes for the soft skills you need to improve.

Soft Skills

❑ Kind

❑ Helpful

❑ Honest

❑ Friendly

❑ Upbeat

❑ Caring

❑ Thoughtful

❑ Patient

❑ Respectful

❑ Sharing

❑ Hardworking

❑ Cooperative

❑ Responsible

❑ Organized

❑ Good communicator

❑ Good self-control

*It is **positive** to be able to tell someone what you are good at and what you are not so good at.* You need to be able to describe your strengths and weaknesses with a vocational counselor or another person who is helping you to find a great job. Also, you will need to be able to describe your strengths to a potential employer so he or she knows why it would be good to hire you. Fill in the blanks below to describe at least two strengths and two weaknesses, and circle the best describing word for them ("somewhat," "quite," or "very" good/weak). Make sure at least one of your strengths is a soft one. Those are the strengths that an employer will most want to know about.

Strengths:

I am _____ (somewhat/quite/very) good at _____ .

I am _____ (somewhat/quite/very) good at _____ .

Weaknesses:

I am _____ (somewhat/quite/very) weak at _____ .

I am _____ (somewhat/quite/very) weak at _____ .

*It is **positive** to develop your soft skill strengths because they are the most important for getting and keeping a job.* Everyone has areas they need to improve. It is positive to set goals for your-self and to focus on areas where you can improve. Check at least two of the boxes for the soft skills from the list below that you want to improve on.

❑ Kind

❑ Helpful

❑ Honest

❑ Friendly

❑ Upbeat

❑ Caring

❑ Thoughtful

❑ Patient

❑ Respectful

❑ Sharing

❑ Hardworking

❑ Cooperative

❑ Responsible

❑ Organized

❑ Good communicator

❑ Good self-control

*It is **positive** to know what to do to improve a skill.* Think about the soft skills you checked off that need improvement. Pick one and write it down.

I want to improve _____.

Practice leads to improvement! Think about a way that you can practice or get help for that soft skill so it can get stronger. Look at the list below to see if anything there might help you. Check the ones from the list that might help or write your own way to improve on the following lines.

It would help me to improve if...

_____

_____.

Things that might help you:

❑ You work on the activities in the sections of this book.

❑ Someone shows you how to do it right.

❑ You make a plan to practice it (when, where, how often).

❑ You write yourself a reminder and put it where you will see it.

❑ Someone shows you what it looks like.

❑ Someone helps you pick tools or supplies for it.

❑ Someone takes a picture of the right way or draws it for you.

❑ You take a picture of the right way or draw it.

❑ Someone reminds you to do it (when, how often).

❑ Someone makes a secret signal to you, so you know to do it.

❑ You write out the steps to achieving success with the skill and do each one.

❑ You think of times you can practice that skill.

*It is **positive** to know what to do to improve a second skill.* Think about the soft strengths you checked off that need improvement. Pick a second one and write it down.

I want to improve _____.

Think about what might help you to improve on that soft strength. Look at the list below to see if anything there might help you. Check which ones from the list that might help or write your own way to improve on the following lines.

It would help me to improve if...

_____

_____.

Things that might help you:

❑ You work on the activities in the sections of this book.

❑ Someone shows you how to do it right.

❑ You make a plan to practice it (when, where, how often).

❑ You write yourself a reminder and put it where you will see it.

❑ Someone shows you what it looks like.

❑ Someone helps you pick tools or supplies for it.

❑ Someone takes a picture of the right way or draws it for you.

❑ You take a picture of the right way or draw it.

❑ Someone reminds you to do it (when, how often).

❑ Someone makes a secret signal to you, so you know to do it.

❑ You write out the steps to achieving success with the skill and do each one.

❑ You think of times you can practice that skill.

*It is **positive** to know how to encourage yourself to increase your confidence when you are doing something that you are not very good at yet.* Your boss might ask you to do something new or in a different way that you don't feel confident about. He or she will want to see that you are self-confident and willing to try. You can improve your confidence with positive self-talk. You are your best supporter! Think of two things that you can say to encourage yourself. See the suggestions below and pick your two favorites, or make up your own. Write them here:

1. _____

_____.

2. _____

_____.

Things you can say to encourage yourself:

❑ I can do it!

❑ I will learn a lot by doing this.

❑ My boss will be impressed with me when I get good at this.

❑ It will be over soon.

❑ It's going to get easier.

❑ Practice makes perfect!

❑ I can stand it for a little while longer.

❑ If I can just get through this part, then the rest is easier.

❑ I can take a break and then come back to it.

❑ I can talk to someone and they can help me out.

❑ I can write it out and follow the directions.

*It is **positive** to look and sound confident even if you are feeling uncomfortable.* Bosses want to hire employees who are confident in the workplace. That means you have to speak confidently and match that with your voice tone and face, even though you may be feeling uncomfortable. This is not being "insincere" or "fake," it is a sincere effort to blend in, make others comfortable, and practice an important skill!

1. Check out the following situations. Choose the confident response.

   Your boss asks you to stock the shelves of the biggest department in the store with only one other person. You think you might not be able to do it. What is a positive response?

   ❑ "I don't think I can do that."

   ❑ "I will give it a try!"

Your boss said that he is giving you extra work because you are such a good worker. You don't feel like you can handle the extra work. What is a positive response?

   ❑ "I can't do more work."

   ❑ "Sure thing, I will get it done."

Your boss wants you to work faster to get clothes unpacked at the store because the store will open soon. You feel under a lot of pressure. What is a positive response?

   ❑ "I can't work any faster! There are too many of them!"

   ❑ "I will do it!"

2. Practice saying the three positive responses that you just checked in front of a mirror. Make sure that your voice tone and your facial expression are upbeat and confident!

*It is **positive** to practice encouraging yourself to keep trying when you are doing something that you are not very good at yet.* If you get in the habit of encouraging yourself any time you are doing something new and different, you may find that it helps you keep trying and not give up.

Pick something that is a little hard for you to do right or very well independently at home (e.g., make your bed, fold clothes, cook a meal all by yourself), and try to do it today. Ask a parent or trusted person for an idea of something you can do. Practice saying something encouraging—more than once—to yourself while you are doing it (you might use the encouraging statements you wrote in 9!).

What I did:

_____

_____

_____.

What I said to encourage myself:

_____

_____

_____.

It is **positive** to recognize and say how you are feeling when you make mistakes, or think you might. It feels uncomfortable to make mistakes, or to think that you might. When you can't do something well or right the first time, what is an "uncomfortable feeling" word that really describes how you feel?*

"When I can't do something right or something is hard for me, then I feel

_____."*

Examples of Uncomfortable Feelings		
Sad	Worried	Lonely
Annoyed	Scared	Anxious
Angry	Disappointed	Hurt
Frustrated	Tired	Overwhelmed
Irritable(Grouchy)	Furious	Bored
Hopeless	Nervous	Ignored
Embarrassed	Hungry	Confused

* Remember: to grow and learn, you sometimes have to be uncomfortable, especially in the beginning (see Step 101). But it gets better and more comfortable as you keep doing it! It takes practice to become comfortable.

*It is **positive** to know helpful ways to cope with uncomfortable feelings when you are in situations where you make mistakes (or think you might) or you have weaker skills.*

Look at the scale below. When you are feeling uncomfortable at a 3 or 4 level, you may need to have positive ways to cope or work through those uncomfortable feelings.

Feeling Uncomfortable ...				
0	**1**	**2**	**3**	**4**
0 = Not at all	1 = A little	2 = Somewhat	3 = Quite a bit	4 = Very

It is **positive** to cope with uncomfortable feelings by:

- Speaking to someone about it
- Taking a walk
- Playing with your pet
- Writing it down
- Listening to music
- Reading a book
- Etc.

There are many ways that people deal with feeling uncomfortable! Write down two **positive** ways that YOU can cope when you feel "quite a bit" or "very" uncomfortable.

_____

_____

_____

_____

_____.

*It is **positive** to have perspective on the strengths and weaknesses of others as well as yourself.* Think about people who know in your home or that you have met in a workplace. Check at least one box for a strength you have noticed for another person, and one for a weakness. Then fill in the blanks below to tell where you noticed that strength and weakness.

❏ Kind   ❏ Respectful

❏ Helpful   ❏ Sharing

❏ Honest   ❏ Hardworking

❏ Friendly   ❏ Cooperative

❏ Upbeat   ❏ Responsible

❏ Caring   ❏ Organized

❏ Thoughtful   ❏ Good communicator

❏ Patient   ❏ Good self-control

The strength I noticed was: _____.

What happened was: _____

_____.

The weakness I noticed was: _____.

What happened was: _____

_____.

*It is **positive** to let people know that you notice what they are good at.* Just as it is positive for you to be able to describe your strengths, it is also positive for you to notice and describe what others are good at. They might notice what you are good at, too!

Tell the person whose strength you noticed in #12 that you notice they are good at _____

_____

and you think it is awesome/great/fantastic/admirable/inspiring/important/amazing (pick one, or think of your own adjective)!*

What I said:

_____

_____

_____.

The person I said it to was:

_____.

* Everyone has weaknesses as well as strengths, and it is often helpful when you can describe your own weaknesses and advocate for your needs. *But it is usually **not positive** or helpful to talk about something that someone else is **not good** at.* If you stick to saying what others are good at, you will show respect for them, and that is good for your reputation!

It is **positive** to respond respectfully when you are corrected. Sometimes a boss/teacher/job coach/vocational counselor/teacher/parent needs to point out a mistake you made, or show you something you can't do yet, so that you can improve. *Anyone* doing a job needs to learn to do new things and may make a mistake and get a correction sometimes. You might, too! It is their job to correct you when you make a mistake so you can do it better next time, and it is **your** job to respond with **positivity**. This means that you look positive, sound positive, use positive words when you speak to them, and do the thing they are asking you to do. This shows respect and helps you to have a good reputation. You will keep jobs (and friendships) if you do this.

There are **positive** things that you can say when you are corrected or given something to do that is hard. Suppose your boss told you that you did something wrong at work, or he asks you to do something you think is hard. Look in the mirror and practice saying aloud each of the following sentences, just as if you are speaking to your boss. *Make sure that your voice and your face are upbeat, friendly, and calm.* Then check the boxes to show that you said them positively.

"Thank you for telling me."	☐ I *sounded* positive	☐ I *looked* positive
"I will work on that."	☐ I *sounded* positive	☐ I *looked* positive
"I will do that better next time."	☐ I *sounded* positive	☐ I *looked* positive
"Can you show me how to do that?"	☐ I *sounded* positive	☐ I *looked* positive
"I am confused; I have a question."	☐ I *sounded* positive	☐ I *looked* positive
"I need to do better with that."	☐ I *sounded* positive	☐ I *looked* positive
"I'm sure I can do it with practice."	☐ I *sounded* positive	☐ I *looked* positive
"I hope I will do it right next time."	☐ I *sounded* positive	☐ I *looked* positive
"I appreciate your help with this."	☐ I *sounded* positive	☐ I *looked* positive

*It is **positive** to encourage yourself when you are corrected.* A boss might point out a mistake you made, or show you something you can't do well yet, so that you can improve at your job and do it better. This happens to everyone in the workplace, and anyone might feel discouraged, embarrassed, or frustrated when it happens. Below, write two encouraging, positive things that you might say to yourself when someone corrects you. (For example: "I will do better next time," and "It will be hard at first but after I do it a few times I will be fine.")

1. _____

_____

_____

_____

_____.

2. _____

_____

_____

_____

_____.

---

*It is **positive** to have perspective on your mistakes and weaknesses at work. You can respond to any problem positively if you have perspective on it or see it within the context of all the various problems in the workplace.*

Suppose your boss tells you that you did something wrong, or she asks you to do something you think you can't do. To help you get perspective, consider what kind of problem this is. Put a check mark beside the categories that you think fit this kind of problem. (The correct answer is below!)

❑ 1. "Oh well, these things just happen!"

❑ 2. "That's okay, it was just an accident."

❑ 3. "It's just hard ..."

❑ 4. "Whoops, my mistake!"

❑ 5. "It was on purpose to hurt or bother me!"

Correct Answer:

- It is correct to check any or all of the first four categories of problems! It is **positive** to not blame yourself or others when you make mistakes, corrections, or have to do something hard or new. That is a positive perspective!

- It is not positive, and it is not appropriate, to see corrections by your boss (or your job coach, your vocational counselor, your parents), as "on purpose to hurt or bother" you. That is also true if they ask you to do something that you think is too hard or that you think you can't do. The reason is that they are doing their job by helping you to develop and grow.

It is **positive** to practice "blending in" with others, or doing what everyone else is doing, even if you are feeling uncomfortable. With practice, you will improve the skill of blending. It is very important in the workplace to be part of the group and to keep doing your job, even if you are feeling uncomfortable. For example, if your boss/teacher/job coach/etc. says you did something wrong or you must do something you think is too hard, you might be feeling hurt, worried, embarrassed, or frustrated. But if you continue to "blend" with others, and keep "going with the flow," that will increase your reputation and others will see you are dependable and calm.

Practice "blending":

1. Go to a place where there are other people. This might be the mall, a store, a party, your place of employment, your church, an activity center, a gym, or your home!

2. Notice the things others are doing, and do those things, too.

3. Notice the expressions on their faces, their overall "body language," and the things they are talking about. Try to copy them.

Write about where you went and how you "blended."

_____

_____

_____

_____

_____

_____

_____.

*It is **positive** to think about and plan for how you will "blend" with others at work when you are feeling uncomfortable.*

If you have strong uncomfortable feelings at work because you made a mistake or have to do something hard, describe how you will "go with the flow" anyway and "blend" with the other workers.

_____

_____

_____

_____

_____

_____

_____

_____.

*It is **positive** to have positive or neutral body language when you are having problems doing something (or are worried you might!).* When you feel frustrated or embarrassed at work, you need to focus to maintain positive body language. This is respectful to others and shows you are dependable, calm, and focused at work. That's good for your reputation!

Circle the numbers that show a neutral or positive body:

1. Jumping up and down

2. Stomping your foot

3. Head up

4. Straight posture

5. Grabbing your head with your hands

6. Calm arms, hands, and legs

7. Throwing your arms out

8. Twisting and bending your body

9. Swinging your arms

10. Head down

11. Twisting and bending down and away from others

12. Eye contact

13. Friendly, calm facial expression

Answers: 3, 4, 6, 12, 13

*It is **positive** to have appropriate voice tone and volume when you are having problems doing something (or are worried you might!).* When you feel frustrated or embarrassed at work, you need to focus to maintain positive and appropriate voice tone and volume. This is respectful to others and shows you are dependable, calm, and focused at work. That's good for your reputation!

Circle the numbers for appropriate voice tone and volume (loudness) when you are having problems doing something (or are worried you might!).

1. Yelling

2. Inside voice

3. Calm voice

4. Complaining voice

5. Whining

6. Respectful voice

Answers: 2, 3, 6

THINGS THAT GO WRONG AND POSITIVITY

Sometimes things just go wrong! When that happens, anyone might feel frustrated, angry, worried, or embarrassed, and find it difficult to be positive. It may be especially hard for individuals with autism when things go wrong. Suppose you spilled something you were carrying. Suppose someone borrows then loses a tool you needed to do your job. Suppose you missed a step in your job and you have to start over again. *When things go wrong, it is **positive** to have perspective on your problem, to have feelings that are appropriate for the kind of problem you are having, and to do and say the right thing for your type of problem.* Staying positive when you have a problem is very important for work and for relationships with others. With practice, you can do it! This section has twenty ways to practice positive steps toward independence and employment if you frequently get angry, frustrated, or very anxious when ...

- "Accidents" or unexpected events occur

- Things that "just happen" in life occur due to circumstances or chance

- Negative things happen because people aren't perfect and make mistakes

*It is **positive** to say something appropriate when things "just happen."* This kind of problem is no one's fault, and it is **positive** to not blame anyone for it. Things might "just happen" because of the circumstance/environment you are in; for example, you might be expected to do a job at work because it has to get done, and that is a normal expectation in the workplace. Also, circumstances can change unexpectedly; for example, you are given a job to do and you can't do it because the equipment broke down! *It is **positive** to recognize that these kinds of problems are no one's fault, and to say something positive when they happen.*

A. Put a check mark by the **positive** things to say after each problem.

B. Put an X by each sentence that is **not positive**. *Remember, when "these things just happen," it is no one's fault and it is not appropriate or positive to blame others.* Make sure your words are appropriate and positive! This makes people comfortable with you and shows respect.

- The menu at the cafeteria at work changed and they don't have what you always order there.
    - ❑ "Oh well, these things just happen!"
    - ❑ "I don't like this place."
    - ❑ "Maybe I can find a new food I like here."

- You like to play video games on Saturday, but on this Saturday you have to work.
    - ❑ "They always ruin my day!"
    - ❑ "Oh well, these things just happen!"
    - ❑ "I can play games later."

- You wanted to do one job at work, but your boss assigned you a different one.
    - ❑ "Sure thing!"
    - ❑ "Oh well, these things just happen!"
    - ❑ "That's not my job and I don't want to do it."

- Your boss wants you to do your job tasks in a different order, but you are comfortable with the way you were doing it before.
    - ❑ "Oh well, these things just happen!"
    - ❑ "You are always messing up my life!"
    - ❑ "I will give it a try."

- At work, you didn't finish your job by the end of the day, so your boss asks you to stay a little later to get it finished.
    - ❑ "It's not fair!"
    - ❑ "Oh well, these things just happen!"
    - ❑ "No problem."

*It is **positive** to do something that 1) "goes with the flow" or is "flexible," and 2) "blends" with or matches others around you when "things just happen."* Just as it is positive to say "Oh well, these things just happen!" whenever circumstances are complicated or when they change, you can also do something positive. It makes others feel comfortable and respected when you are flexible and "blend" in with them after a problem.

Put a check mark in front of the positive thing to do for each problem. Put an X by actions that are **not positive**. Remember:

1. When things "just happen," it is no one's fault, so don't blame anyone!

2. It is positive to be "flexible" or to "go with the flow."

3. Consider what others around you are doing so you can match them and "blend."

• The menu at the cafeteria at work changed and they don't have what you always order there. You ...

    ❑ Pick something different from the menu.

    ❑ Refuse to eat at the restaurant.

    ❑ Blame the restaurant for changing the menu.

• You like to play video games on Saturday, but on this Saturday you have to work. You ...

    ❑ Go to your room and close the door.

    ❑ Refuse to go to work.

    ❑ Plan to play the games later or on another day.

• You wanted to do one job at work, but your boss assigned you a different one. You ...

    ❑ Quit your job.

    ❑ Do the work your boss gives you.

    ❑ Refuse to do the new job.

• Your boss wants you to do your job tasks in a different order, but you are comfortable with the way you were doing it before. You ...

    ❑ Do them in the order you like to do them.

    ❑ Say, "Sure thing!" and do them the way your boss asks you to do them.

    ❑ Stop coming to work.

• At work, you didn't finish your job by the end of the day, so your boss asks you to stay a little later to get it finished. You ...

    ❑ Go home anyway.

    ❑ Say, "It's not fair, you can do it yourself!"

    ❑ Stay and get the work done.

*It is **positive** to **say** something appropriate when things happen accidentally.* This kind of problem happens unexpectedly and is no one's fault, so it is **positive** to be forgiving and helpful when it happens! It is rare for people to do things on purpose to hurt or bother you, so assume it was just an accident and be positive!

A. Put a check mark by the **positive things to say** after each problem.

B. Put an X by each sentence that is **not positive**. *Remember, when an accident happens, it was not done on purpose to hurt or bother you, so it is not appropriate or positive to blame someone.* Make sure your words are appropriate and **positive**! This makes people comfortable with you and shows respect.

• Someone bumped into you at work and you spilled what you were carrying.

❑ "That's okay, it was just an accident."

❑ "Watch what you are doing!"

❑ "No problem, you didn't mean to do it."

• Someone accidentally erased what you had on the computer.

❑ "That's okay, it was just an accident."

❑ "You idiot! Why did you do that?"

❑ "I have done that, too; don't worry about it."

• Someone accidentally gave you the wrong directions and you got lost.

❑ "You made me get lost!"

❑ "That's okay, it was just an accident."

❑ "You didn't mean to do it."

• Someone called you by the wrong name and said "I'm sorry" when you told them your correct name.

❑ "I already told you once."

❑ "You should know my name by now."

❑ "That's okay. No problem."

• Someone accidentally took your uniform at work and wore it.

❑ "Hey, you stole my uniform!"

❑ "That's okay, it was just an accident."

❑ "No problem, you didn't mean to do it."

*It is **positive** to **do** something that 1) "goes with the flow" or is "flexible," and 2) "blends" with or matches others around you when something happens by accident.* After you say, "That's okay, it was just an accident," then you follow it up with an appropriate action. It makes others feel comfortable and respected when you are flexible and "go with the flow" after a problem.

Put a check mark in front of the **positive thing to do** for each problem. Put an X by actions that are **not positive**. Remember:

1. When something happens that was an accident, it is no one's fault, so don't blame anyone!

2. It is positive to be "flexible" or to "go with the flow."

3. Consider what others around you are doing so you can match them and "blend."

• Someone bumped into you at work and you spilled what you were carrying.

    ❑ You push them back.

    ❑ You pick up what was spilled and continue on.

    ❑ You smile in a friendly way and say, "It's okay, it was just an accident."

• Someone accidentally erased what you had on the computer.

    ❑ You sit down to see if you can retrieve the information.

    ❑ You pound your fist on the computer.

    ❑ You start over if you need to.

• Someone accidentally gave you the wrong directions and you got lost.

    ❑ You refuse to talk to that person again.

    ❑ You ask someone else for directions.

    ❑ You check your phone or a map to figure out where you are and continue in the right direction.

• Someone called you by the wrong name.

    ❑ You politely let them know your correct name.

    ❑ You just move on and continue to do what you were doing.

    ❑ You make an unfriendly face and move away from the person.

• Someone accidentally took your uniform at work and wore it.

    ❑ You check and make sure that your uniforms are not mixed in with others for next time.

    ❑ You go tell your boss that your co-worker took your uniform.

    ❑ You continue to be friendly and positive to that person at work.

*It is **positive** to **say** something appropriate when you make a mistake that causes a problem.* Everyone makes mistakes! If you caused a problem by mistake, you can say, "Whoops, my mistake, I will try harder next time!" and then do your best to fix the problem you caused. That is responsible, respectful to others, and will give you a good reputation at work and with your friends.

A. Put a check mark by the **positive** things to say after each problem.

B. Put an X by each action that is **not positive**. *Remember, when you make a mistake and it causes a problem, others will understand (or should understand) that it was not done on purpose, so do not be too hard on yourself. Everyone makes mistakes!*

People don't care if you are perfect—they *do* care if you are *positive*!

• You overslept and you were late to work for the first time ever.

    ❑ "I'm very sorry, I won't let that happen again."

    ❑ "It's stupid to start work this early, anyway."

    ❑ "Whoops, my mistake; I will make sure to set my alarm next time."

• You work with animals and you were talking loudly to a co-worker. You scared the animals, and a few escaped from their pens.

    ❑ "I was just talking, I wasn't that loud!"

    ❑ "I'm very sorry, can I help to catch the ones that got away?"

    ❑ "I will not be loud around the animals again."

• You were too slow on the assembly line and they had to stop it so you could catch up.

    ❑ "I'm sorry, I will try to work faster."

    ❑ "Can you give me some pointers about how I can work faster at my station?"

    ❑ "The line moves too fast; you should slow it down, it's impossible!"

• You forgot to bring all the things that the boss told you to go get, now everyone does not have the tools they need to start their work.

    ❑ "Whoops, I'm sorry. I will go back and get the rest of the things!"

    ❑ "You didn't write it down, it was impossible to remember all that!"

    ❑ "I'm sorry, I will write everything down next time so I don't forget anything."

*It is **positive** to **do** something whenever you make a mistake that 1) shows you take responsibility for the mistake you made, 2) shows you can "go with the flow" and be "flexible" to keep on working and being with others.* It helps others understand your mistake was an accident when you speak and act positively.

Put a check mark in front of the **positive things to do** for each problem. Put an X by each action that is **not positive**. Remember, when you make a mistake and it causes a problem, others will understand (or should understand) that it was not done on purpose, so do not be too hard on yourself. Everyone makes mistakes!

People don't care if you are perfect, they *do* care if you are *positive*!

- You overslept and you were late to work for the first time ever.

    ❑ Get mad at the early start time and quit the job.

    ❑ Ask someone at home to check to make sure you are up in time for work.

    ❑ Set two alarms, just to be sure you wake up.

- You work with animals, and you were talking loudly to a co-worker. You scared the animals, and a few escaped from their pens.

    ❑ Speak quietly or not at all from now on when you are around the animals.

    ❑ Refuse to help get the animals back because you did nothing wrong.

    ❑ Help to recapture the animals that escaped.

- You were too slow on the assembly line and they had to stop it so you could catch up.

    ❑ Practice and get help for moving quicker and being more efficient on the line.

    ❑ Talk to your vocational counselor to see if this job is really a good fit for your work speed.

    ❑ Get mad and quit the job.

- You forgot to bring all the things that the boss told you to go get, now everyone does not have the tools they need to start their work.

    ❑ Make them go get their own.

    ❑ Offer to go back and bring everything that is needed.

    ❑ Write a list of things needed so you don't forget next time.

*It is **positive** to **say** something appropriate when things are "just hard."* For example, when someone you love becomes ill or dies, or you break up with a boyfriend or girlfriend, or you are having a hard time doing a difficult task, you may struggle to say and do positive things.

A. Put a check mark by the **positive** things to say after each problem.

B. Put an X by each sentence that is **not positive**. Make sure your words are appropriate and **positive**! This makes people comfortable around you.

• Your grandmother is sick, and you are worried about her.

- ❑ "This work is stupid, I don't want to be here."
- ❑ "I can call her later to check how she is."
- ❑ "It's just hard for me to focus on what I am doing today."

• You had a friend who won't talk to you now.

- ❑ "It's really hard for me now that you won't talk to me."
- ❑ "I can do something I enjoy to take my mind off my friend."
- ❑ "I can't stand her anyway."

• You have to pull weeds and bushes at the park and dig fence post holes, and it is very slow and hard work.

- ❑ "This is a really hard job, but I can do it."
- ❑ "Just a few more and we will be done."
- ❑ "This is impossible."

*It is **positive** to **do** something when things are hard that 1) "goes with the flow" or is "flexible," and 2) "blends" with or matches others around you.* For example, when someone you love becomes ill or dies, or you break up with a boyfriend or girlfriend, or you are having a hard time doing a difficult task, you may struggle to say and do positive things.

A. Put a check mark by the **positive** things to do after each problem.

B. Put an X by each action that is **not positive**. Make sure your actions are appropriate and positive! This makes people comfortable with you and shows respect.

• Your grandmother is sick, and you are worried about her.

    ❑ Stop showing up at your job until she is better.

    ❑ Let your boss know that you are going through a rough time at home.

    ❑ Try to stay focused on doing your job while you are there, plan to contact Grandmother later to check on her.

• You had a friend who won't talk to you now.

    ❑ Tell someone you trust how you are feeling.

    ❑ Frown and don't answer people who speak to you.

    ❑ Write a positive text or email to your friend asking to meet and talk about it.

• You have to pull weeds and bushes at the park and dig fence post holes, and it is very slow and hard work.

    ❑ Take a lot of breaks.

    ❑ Work as hard as everyone else is working.

    ❑ Be a team player and help everyone get done as fast as you all can.

*It is **positive** to keep a calm and friendly face and voice when you have problems.* Look in the mirror and practice saying aloud each of the following sentences, just as if you are speaking to your boss, a co-worker, a friend, or a family member. ***Make sure that your voice and your face are upbeat, friendly, and calm.*** Then check the boxes to show that you said them positively.

"That's okay, it was just an accident!" ❑ I *sounded* positive ❑ I *looked* positive

"These things just happen." ❑ I *sounded* positive ❑ I *looked* positive

"It's okay, you didn't mean to do it." ❑ I *sounded* positive ❑ I *looked* positive

"My mistake. I will do better next time." ❑ I *sounded* positive ❑ I *looked* positive

"Sure thing, I will fix that right now." ❑ I *sounded* positive ❑ I *looked* positive

"No problem." ❑ I *sounded* positive ❑ I *looked* positive

"It's not your fault." ❑ I *sounded* positive ❑ I *looked* positive

"I don't blame you." ❑ I *sounded* positive ❑ I *looked* positive

"It happens—no big deal." ❑ I *sounded* positive ❑ I *looked* positive

When things go wrong, we all feel uncomfortable! *It is **positive** to recognize how you are feeling and to be able to say it to a trusted person.* When something goes wrong, what is an "uncomfortable feeling" word that really describes how you feel? That depends what kind of problem it is! Check out the list of "uncomfortable feelings" below and find the appropriate feeling for a few of the problem situations we considered before. You might have more than one feeling about each one!

Examples of Uncomfortable Feelings

Sad	Worried	Lonely
Annoyed	Scared	Anxious
Angry	Disappointed	Hurt
Frustrated	Tired	Overwhelmed
Irritable (Grouchy)	Furious	Bored
Hopeless	Nervous	Ignored
Embarrassed	Hungry	Confused

You overslept and you were late to work for the first time ever. You feel ...

_____

Someone accidentally erased everything you did on the computer. You feel ...

_____

You wanted to do one job at work, but your boss assigned you a different one. You feel ...

_____

* It is also **positive** to avoid expressing anger when a problem has happened by accident, or because you or another person made a mistake, or because "these things just happen!" People aren't perfect, so no matter what happens, please remember that your positivity is truly the most important thing to your boss, coworkers, and friends.

Look at the scale below. When you are feeling uncomfortable at a 3 or 4 level, you may need to have **positive** ways to cope or deal with those uncomfortable feelings.*

Feeling Uncomfortable ...				
0	**1**	**2**	**3**	**4**
0 = Not at all	1 = A little	2 = Somewhat	3 = Quite a bit	4 = Very

It is **positive** to cope with uncomfortable feelings by:

- Speaking to someone about it
- Taking a walk
- Playing with your pet
- Writing it down
- Listening to music
- Reading a book
- Etc.

There are *many* ways that people deal with feeling uncomfortable! Write down two **positive** ways that YOU can cope when you feel "quite a bit" or "very" uncomfortable.

1. _____

    _____

    _____.

2. _____

    _____

    _____.

---

* It is also **positive** to have **appropriate** perspective and intensity of feeling about your problem. Discuss with a trusted person: how appropriate is the intensity of your feeling for the kind of problem it is? What is an appropriate intensity for this problem? Pick someone that you know very well—how would he or she feel about each of the problems? Is it different than how you would feel?

*It is **positive** to "blend" with others, no matter how you are feeling on the inside.* That means that you do what everyone else is doing and keep on with the job! That creates a positive reputation for you and makes others feel respected. If something goes wrong and you feel very uncomfortable, you might be tempted to "do your own thing." But the appropriate, **positive** thing to do at work (and anytime you are with others) is to check out what everyone else is doing, then "blend" in and match them, and keep "going with the flow!"

Let's consider a few previous "problem situations" and two possible actions. Which one is "blending"?

- You overslept and you were late to work for the first time ever.

    ❑ Complain about the early start time and quit the job.

    ❑ Do your best at work that day and make sure to set your alarm for the next day.

- Someone bumped into you at work and you spilled what you were carrying.

    ❑ You push them back.

    ❑ You pick up what was spilled and continue on.

- Someone accidentally erased what you had on the computer.

    ❑ You sit down to see if you can retrieve the information.

    ❑ You pound your fist on the computer.

- The menu at your favorite restaurant changed and they don't have what you always order there.

    ❑ You pick something different from the menu.

    ❑ You refuse to eat at the restaurant.

- You wanted to do one job at work, but your boss assigned you a different one.

    ❑ Do the work your boss gives you.

    ❑ Refuse to do the new job and quit.

*It is **positive** to encourage yourself to keep going, and to "blend" when problems happen because you make a mistake that causes problems for yourself or others.* Below, write two encouraging, positive things that you might say to yourself when **you** make a mistake that causes problems for yourself or others.

When I make a mistake that causes a problem for myself or others, I can say to myself:

_____

_____

_____

_____

_____

_____ .

Or I can say:

_____

_____

_____

_____

_____

_____ .

*It is **positive** to encourage yourself to keep going with the flow, and to "blend" when problems happen for you because others make mistakes.* Below, write two encouraging, positive things that you might say to yourself when **others** make mistakes and that causes problems for you.*

When someone I work (or live) with makes a mistake that causes a problem for me, I can say to myself:

_____

_____

_____

_____

_____

_____.

Or I can say:

_____

_____

_____

_____

_____

_____.

* Remember that people aren't perfect, so no matter what happens, always remember that your positivity is truly the most important thing to your boss, coworkers, and friends.

*It is **positive** to encourage yourself to "go with the flow" and to "blend in" with others when problems happen because of the circumstances or situation.* Below, write two encouraging, positive things that you might say to yourself when you are in a situation that is uncomfortable for you.

When problems happen because of the circumstances or situation, I can say to myself:

_____

_____

_____

_____

_____

_____.

Or I can say:

_____

_____

_____

_____

_____

_____.

It is **positive** to encourage yourself to "go with the flow" and to "blend in" with others when problems happen because the circumstances **change unexpectedly**. Below, write two encouraging, positive things that you might say to yourself *when circumstances* **change unexpectedly**.

When a situation changes and I didn't expect it, I can say to myself:

_____

_____

_____

_____

_____

_____

_____.

Or I can say:

_____

_____

_____

_____

_____

_____

_____.

It is **positive** to encourage yourself so that you can continue to "go with the flow" and "blend" when problems happen **because something is "just hard."** Below, write two encouraging, positive things that you might say to yourself *when something happens that is hard.* Look at numbers 27 and 28 for examples of things that are hard.

When things are "just hard," I can say to myself:

_____

_____

_____

_____

_____

_____.

Or I can say:

_____

_____

_____

_____

_____

_____.

*It is **positive** to express your problems with the appropriate person, at the appropriate time and place.* When we experience problems, it is usually positive to talk about them with others. But we must be careful how we share them in order to be respectful and to have a good reputation. Put a check next to the answer with the appropriate person, time, and place to share or talk about the following problem. Put an X beside the one that is **not** appropriate or positive.

• Problem: You wanted to do one job at work, but your boss assigned you a different one.

  ❑ Ask to speak privately to your boss when he has a moment. When he comes to speak to you, say (in a positive voice), "I hope I am doing a good job with _____, but I would love to do _____ instead. Is there any chance for me to do that?" (And be positive, no matter what his response is!)

  ❑ Call your vocational counselor. Tell her that you would like to try a different job than the one you currently have. Can she help you?

  ❑ Talk to your boss in front of other people while he is doing something else and tell him, "I don't want to do that job! Do I have to? I'd rather do _____," in a complaining voice.

"Tact" means saying something that you need to say very carefully, so you do not offend or embarrass someone else. Not offending or embarrassing others is very important for your reputation and it also shows respect for others. Being tactful is not being "insincere" or "fake," it is a sincere effort to make others comfortable, and this is an important social skill!

*It is **positive** to speak tactfully to coworkers, bosses, and customers at all times when you are at work, even when you are having problems!*

Put a check mark beside the statement that is **tactful**.

- ❏ "I don't want to do this job."
- ❏ "I would really love to do _____ (other job) if there is an opportunity for me to do that sometime."
- ❏ "I don't have enough time to do all that!"
- ❏ "Is it possible for me to have a little extra time to get it all done?"
- ❏ "That's a dumb way to do it."
- ❏ "Can you please explain to me why we do it that way?"
- ❏ "It's impossible for one person to do this job!"
- ❏ "Will anyone be able to help me get this done?"

It is **positive** to accept what your supervisor/boss/job coach says to you, even if it doesn't change or improve the problem you are having. When you are on the job you need to accept directives, answers, etc. that are not what you want to hear, and may not solve a problem you are having. To have a positive relationship and show respect to an authority figure, you need to stay positive in these situations.

1. Put a check mark by the positive thing to say and do for each situation.

- You say to your boss, "I would really love to do _____ (other job) if there is an opportunity for me to do that sometime," and your boss says, "No, sorry, I need you to continue doing the job I gave you."

    ❑ You say, "I quit!" and leave.

    ❑ You say, "Sure thing," and go back to work.

- You say to your boss, "Is it possible for me to have a little extra time to get it all done?" Your boss says, "No, I need it all done by 5:00."

    ❑ You say, "That's impossible!" and get mad.

    ❑ You say, "I will do my best," and then you work extra hard and fast.

- You say, "Will anyone be able to help me get this done?" Your boss says, "Sorry, I don't have anyone else I can put with you to help get it done."

    ❑ You say, "It's impossible for one person to do this job!" and sit down, looking angry.

    ❑ You say, "Okay, I will get it done," and then you work extra hard and fast.

2. Look in the mirror. Try saying the positive things you marked above with a positive voice tone and facial expression. Check the boxes below to show that you did it.

❑ I *sounded* positive   ❑ I *looked* positive

WORD CHOICES AND POSITIVITY

A lot of your positivity at work and with friends is expressed in the words you say. It is challenging for everyone to say the "right thing" when speaking with people, but as an individual with autism you might find that choosing what to say is a particular "positivity challenge" for you. *When you speak to others, it is **positive** to choose the words that will make others feel respected and valued, and that will give you a good reputation as well.*

Suppose you need to tell someone to stop talking so you can do your work, but you don't want to hurt their feelings. Suppose you want a co-worker to like you. Suppose you want to tell someone else how they should do something in a better way without offending them. Suppose you need to report a problem to your boss. There are word choices that you can make to help you get it done *positively*. This section has twenty ways to practice positive steps toward independence and employment, if you struggle to find and use words with others that:

- Are polite

- Are complimentary

- Are encouraging to others

- Show acceptance of others

- Show self-acceptance or positive self-concept

- Solve problems with others

- Are kind

- Are tactful

- Acknowledge and respond to others

- Are framed or structured in a way that shows respect

- Are on an appropriate topic for the workplace

- Are an appropriate length/amount of talking

- Happen at the right time and place, to the right person

- Have positive voice tone and body language to match and support the words

- Are "nice and necessary"

- Share personal/sensitive information privately

- Shift in style from casual to formal as appropriate

It is **positive** to use polite words whenever you ask for something ("please"), when you receive something ("thank you"), when you make a mistake ("excuse me" or "I'm sorry"), and when you are thanked by someone else ("you're welcome"). Polite words need to be used **every time**, for each of these situations. It is not okay to just use them sometimes but not at other times. Speaking politely is a simple thing that you can do to build your reputation and to show respect for others.

- You need your coworker's help with a job. ("Can you please help me?")

- You dropped the frame you were working with and now it won't be ready on time. ("I'm sorry.")

- You bump into another person while they are carrying something. ("Excuse me.")

- You need a certain tool, and you notice a coworker is using one. ("Can I please use that when you're done?")

- Your boss helps you tie a knot in your supply line. ("Thank you.")

- You need to get in your locker at work and two coworkers are standing in front of it talking. ("Excuse me, I need to open my locker.")

It is very important to use a friendly face and a positive voice tone when you are speaking politely. Practice saying the sentences below while you are looking in the mirror. Check the boxes when you sound and look positive while saying them.

"Can you please help me?"	☐ I *sounded* positive	☐ I *looked* positive
"I'm sorry, I forgot to do it."	☐ I *sounded* positive	☐ I *looked* positive
"Excuse me for cutting through here."	☐ I *sounded* positive	☐ I *looked* positive
"Can I please use that when you're done?"	☐ I *sounded* positive	☐ I *looked* positive
"Thank you for all your help on this project."	☐ I *sounded* positive	☐ I *looked* positive
"Excuse me, I need to get in here."	☐ I *sounded* positive	☐ I *looked* positive
"You're very welcome, I am glad to help."	☐ I *sounded* positive	☐ I *looked* positive

*It is also **positive** and polite to frame your sentences in the form of a question instead of a declaration, especially if you are speaking to an authority figure and even when you speak to co-workers.* "Telling" your boss instead of "asking" may make you sound "bossy" or like a "know-it-all," and is not polite. Speaking to authority figures and co-workers with polite questions instead of declarations will enhance your reputation and make others enjoy working with you more.

Change the following declarations into politely formed questions.

Example: Instead of **telling** your boss, "I think we're done here," you should **ask**, "Is there anything more for me to do?" That is positive and polite.

"I'm going to go let in the chickens now," should be:

_____?

"I need the hose (which boss is using)," should be:

_____?

"I'm going to go get the tools for the next job," should be:

_____?

"I don't think we need to pull the weeds here," should be:

_____?

"You do this part and I will do this part over here," should be:

_____?

*It is **positive** to speak kindly to others.* It is most important to speak kindly whenever other people are having trouble with something. It is a way to show other people you care about their issues and challenges. It is **positive** to speak kindly to everyone. You should even speak kindly to people you don't know very well and people you may not like! Speaking kindly shows respect for others and also builds your reputation as a kind and caring person.

Put a check mark by the statement after each situation that is **positive** because it is *kind*.

- Your co-worker locked her keys in her car.
    - ❑ "You should always carry spare keys."
    - ❑ "Can I help?"
- Your boss can't find the papers you typed for him.
    - ❑ "I will help you look."
    - ❑ "Oh no! Really? It took me forever to type those!"
- Your co-worker is worried that the boss doesn't like her.
    - ❑ "You might get fired."
    - ❑ "I'm sure he likes you—you're such a good worker!"
- Your co-worker just came back to work after being gone for a week with an illness.
    - ❑ "I'm glad you are back!"
    - ❑ "I had to do all your work while you were gone."
- Your co-worker is leaving and taking another job because he is moving.
    - ❑ "Can I have your chair and desk?"
    - ❑ "I'm sorry you have to leave, we will miss you."
- Your boss keeps having equipment break down and it is expensive for her to replace it. She is asking everyone to be more careful with the equipment.
    - ❑ "I'm sorry there have been so many problems with the equipment; I will be very careful."
    - ❑ "I didn't do anything to the equipment, it's not my fault."

It is **positive** to look and sound friendly and caring when you say something kind. If your voice tone and face do not match your words, that person might take the words to mean the opposite! Look in the mirror to make sure your face looks positive, friendly, and caring, and check that your voice tone is kind while you say the following sentences. Mark the boxes when you know that you sound and look positive!

"Can I help?" ❑ I *sounded* positive ❑ I *looked* positive

"I will help you look." ❑ I *sounded* positive ❑ I *looked* positive

"I'm glad you are back!" ❑ I *sounded* positive ❑ I *looked* positive

"I'm sorry you've been having problems." ❑ I *sounded* positive ❑ I *looked* positive

"If you need me, just let me know." ❑ I *sounded* positive ❑ I *looked* positive

"I'm here for you." ❑ I *sounded* positive ❑ I *looked* positive

"I hope things work out for you." ❑ I *sounded* positive ❑ I *looked* positive

"I hope you feel better soon." ❑ I *sounded* positive ❑ I *looked* positive

"If there is anything I can do, let me know." ❑ I *sounded* positive ❑ I *looked* positive

*It is **positive** to give someone a compliment when they do something well!* When you give some-one a compliment, it shows that you are noticing that person. Everyone likes to be noticed, es-pecially for something good!* When you give compliments to your boss or co-workers, it builds your reputation as a kind, positive person who would be nice to know.

*Play it safe!

*When you compliment someone, you must **not** make personal comments about their appearance or personal characteristics (pretty/ugly, wrinkled, messy/neat, fat/thin, smart, rich, etc.). Your comments should instead be related to a specific action or product (like doing a good job) by that person.*

Here are some "safe" compliments you can say to someone at work. Say each aloud in front of the mirror. Practice saying them with a positive voice tone and a friendly face.

"Wow, you really made that table shine!"

"I wish you could teach me to do that as well as you do it."

"You got your work done so fast!"

"Thanks, your directions were very clear."

"You really helped me out a lot."

"You set a good example for everyone here."

"I wish I could make that as well as you do!"

"Great job!"

"Nice work!"

❑ I *sounded* positive   ❑ I *looked* positive

*It is **positive** to encourage others when things are hard, or they made a mistake.* You can and should say positive things to let others know that you support them. This will help you to get the job done with your co-workers and have a good reputation.

"You can do it!"

'It's okay, you'll do better next time."

"Don't give up, you'll get it!"

"Good job!"

"Nice try."

"It's a hard one, but you can get it!"

"That happened to me, too."

"I would be happy to help you if I can."

"Please let me know how I can help."

"Only one more!"

"You've almost got it!"

"Wow, that's really tough."

"You are the right person for this job!"

"Don't worry about it, everyone understands."

❑ I *sounded* positive   ❑ I *looked* positive

*It is **positive** to speak tactfully to others*; that means that even when you think something negative, what you say and do is positive. This will avoid hurting the feelings of others, embarrassing them, or sounding rude and bossy. When you say something in a way that won't hurt anyone's feelings or embarrass them, this is **tactful**. Even if you are thinking something negative, you can make your words tactful so you will sound positive. Your voice and face should be pleasant and friendly, too. Speaking tactfully shows respect and increases your reputation; it will make others want to know you and to work with you.

Being tactful is not being "insincere" or "fake," it is a sincere effort to make others comfortable, and this is an important social skill!

Consider the following situations and check the sentences that are **tactful**.

- Your boss asks you to do extra paperwork—a checklist about the team's job tasks—that you think is just extra busy work. The checklist is not helpful and does not even cover the jobs you are doing.
  - ❏ "This checklist is pointless and is a waste of my time."
  - ❏ "I created a checklist that I feel matches our job tasks better, may I use that one instead of this?"
- You were invited to sit with your coworkers at lunch, but you don't want to.
  - ❏ "I'm sorry, I can't today."
  - ❏ "I don't want to sit with you at lunch."
- You think a TV show that your coworker likes is boring and dumb. He asks you if you like that show.
  - ❏ "That's such a dumb and boring show."
  - ❏ "That show is okay, but I like this one better."
- You feel like your boss is always giving you the hardest jobs. He just asked you if you want to do another one.
  - ❏ "Why do I always have to do the hard stuff? Make someone else do it!"
  - ❏ "That's a tough one, but I will do my best."
- You feel you deserve a raise in pay because you have worked at this job for a long time and you have more responsibilities than you used to have.
  - ❏ (At a private time and place with your boss) "I have more responsibilities now at work and I would appreciate a raise in my salary. Is that possible?"
  - ❏ "I don't get paid enough for what I am doing, you should pay me more."

*It is **positive** to use tact, but **sometimes you should say nothing at all** when you are thinking something negative.* Before you say anything, ask yourself if it is *nice* or *necessary* to say it. If it is not nice or necessary, then you say nothing.

Example:

You think your boss or co-worker is doing something inefficiently/wrong. You were not asked for your opinion, but you want to tell him how to do it better ("the right way").

- You are not in charge or responsible for this, and you were not asked for your opinion; it is not necessary to comment, so you *say nothing.*

Example:

You think the uniform you wear at work is ugly and uncomfortable.

- It is part of the job expectation for you to wear this uniform, and everyone else is wearing it, so you must wear it, too. It is not necessary or nice to complain about it, so you *say nothing.*

Example:

You overheard a co-worker tell someone that she can't pay her bills and has declared bankruptcy. You want to tell others about this.

- It is not nice and it is not necessary to share this personal information with others. It was not told to you by this person and you were not given permission to share this personal (and probably embarrassing!) information, so it would not be nice to share it with others. This person did nothing that was illegal or that was wrong related to the job, so it is not necessary to tell others. You should *say nothing.*

Fill in the following blanks:

Before I say anything, I ask myself if it is _____ or

_____ to say it.

If it is not, then I will say _____.

*It is **positive** to speak to the appropriate person at work about a problem.* The appropriate person is someone who can help you solve the problem, will keep the information you share private, and/or who needs to know it because they have responsibilities related to the problem you want to share.

Put a check mark by the person who is probably *least appropriate* to share your problem with, for a ...

1. Problem with the job:
   - ❏ Co-worker
   - ❏ Boss
   - ❏ Job Coach

2. Problem with a co-worker:
   - ❏ Another Co-worker
   - ❏ Boss
   - ❏ Job Coach

3. Problem with negative feelings/anxiety:
   - ❏ Another Co-worker
   - ❏ Vocational Counselor
   - ❏ Job Coach

Consider the description above of an appropriate person to tell your problem to. The appropriate person is someone who can help you solve the problem, will keep the information you share private, and who needs to know it because they have responsibilities related to the problem you want to share.

Answers for 1–3, above: It depends, but generally speaking, the *least* appropriate person may be:

1. A co-worker. Why?_____

2. Another co-worker. Why?_____

3. Another co-worker. Why?_____

*It is **positive** to share personal information privately.* Your body, your feelings, your mental and physical health, your finances, and your concerns or worries are personal. This means you only talk about them in a private place to a person who you trust *and* who is trusted by people who care about you.

Explain to a trusted person at least one problem with sharing personal information ...

On social media:

_____

_____

_____

_____

_____

In an email:

_____

_____

_____

_____

_____

With a group of co-workers:

_____

_____

_____

_____

_____

*It is **positive** to speak at the appropriate time.* Interrupting, blurting out, and talking while you are supposed to be working are examples of **not** speaking at the appropriate time. Please consider the following situations and check the box to show whether or not this is an appropriate time to speak to this person.

- Your co-worker is focused on her work at her computer.

    ❏ Appropriate time to speak to this person.

    ❏ Not an appropriate time to speak to this person.

- Your boss is giving instructions to a group.

    ❏ Appropriate time to speak to this person.

    ❏ Not an appropriate time to speak to this person.

- You are at lunch with co-workers.

    ❏ Appropriate time to speak to these people.

    ❏ Not an appropriate time to speak to these people.

- Someone is in the middle of telling a story to another person.

    ❏ Appropriate time to speak to this person.

    ❏ Not an appropriate time to speak to this person.

- You are leaving work with your co-workers.

    ❏ Appropriate time to speak to these people.

    ❏ Not an appropriate time to speak to these people.

- At the end of the day, your boss says, "Do you have any plans for the weekend?"

    ❏ Appropriate time to speak to this person.

    ❏ Not an appropriate time to speak to this person.

- You and your friend are working at opposite ends of a big room.

    ❏ Appropriate time to speak to this person.

    ❏ Not an appropriate time to speak to this person.

- You and your friend are working side-by-side and your boss said it is okay if you talk quietly while you work.

    ❏ Appropriate time to speak to this person.

    ❏ Not an appropriate time to speak to this person.

*It is **positive** to speak to others in appropriate places.* Often, your main place of work is not an appropriate place to chat with others—unless it is about work-related topics for a short time, or at a designated break or eating place. Also, if you have something private to talk to your boss or supervisor about, you need to do this in a private location.

Find out what the rules are about where you may talk to others at your job, and write them below.

At my job, I can talk to my co-workers in these places:

_____

_____

_____

_____

_____

_____

_____.

A private place to talk to my boss or supervisor would be:

_____

_____

_____

_____

_____

_____

_____.

*It is **positive** to discuss topics that make everyone feel comfortable at work.* At the right time and place, it is also good to talk about things that other people know about and are truly interested in. Good topics to chat about with others at work include the weather, seasons, sports, and what you/they are doing at work. You may possibly chat appropriately with a co-worker about something that you are both interested in, such as games, TV shows, movies, and so forth. (Watch for signs that they are not interested, though, such as looking away, not saying much, or changing the subject. Drop or change the topic if you see those signs!)

- You should **never** talk about these things at work, because they make others uncomfortable: sex, politics, how much money you or others earn, personal/family problems, religion, divisive issues in the news, negative opinions about others—especially co-workers and bosses.

- **Limit** sharing your opinions with others at work, and do not press others to share theirs with you. Many people keep their opinions private.

Check sentences that express appropriate topics and opinions for the workplace. Remember that a positive topic makes others feel comfortable. Answers are below.

- ❑ 1) Did you watch the Super Bowl last night?
- ❑ 2) It hasn't rained for days, and the weatherman says all next week is dry, too!
- ❑ 3) I love Miley Cyrus. I watch all her videos. She is so sexy!
- ❑ 4) My parents just got a divorce and now we don't have enough money to pay our bills.
- ❑ 5) I can't believe it is almost fall. It's almost football season! Do you like football?
- ❑ 6) How much do you earn? I just got a raise, did you?
- ❑ 7) This project they are having us do is really hard. I'm doing a little better with it today, though. How about you?
- ❑ 8) I know everything about the *Titanic*. You don't like the *Titanic*? Well, here are some interesting facts about it: It took more than two years to build it, it had a crew of 900 people, and over 1,500 people died when it sank. It sank on April 15, 1912.
- ❑ 9) Who are you going to vote for in the election? I hate Democrats. You're not voting for them, I hope.
- ❑ 10) Where do you go to church?

***Answer:** Appropriate and positive topics for your workplace are: 1, 2, 5, 7. The other topics are likely to make other people feel uncomfortable.*

*It is **positive** to limit how much you talk at work.*

Which of the following are **true** statements?

- ❑ 1) You are paid to do your job, and talking with others may interfere with your focus or theirs.

- ❑ 2) You can talk to someone working near you while you both work if *it is allowed and if that other person wants to talk while they are working, too.*

- ❑ 3) It is okay if you do most or all of the talking.

- ❑ 4) It is okay to talk about your special interest area at work, even if the other person doesn't look interested (looks away, doesn't say much, tries to change the topic).

- ❑ 5) You can text people even if you aren't allowed to talk.

Answer: *The only **true** statements are 1 and 2. It is **positive** to limit how much you talk at work, even when you are allowed to talk and when the other person shows interest in what you are saying (the other person should talk, too, at least half the time). Texting is seldom allowed at work. Always check with your boss. If you are asked to stop talking, then stop!*

*It is **positive** to express a variety of feeling words, for both your feelings and those of others, so that you can respond to the problems others are having and so you can work through and cope with your own.*

Comfortable feelings: happy, excited, confident, proud, pleased, calm, peaceful, joyful, respected, silly, awesome, loved, cheerful, energetic, determined, hopeful, surprised, upbeat.

Uncomfortable feelings: sad, frustrated, embarrassed disappointed, nervous, anxious, angry, scared, furious, annoyed, irritable, grouchy, worried, tired, hungry, hurt, hopeless, lonely, overwhelmed.

Write something that happened recently that gave you a **comfortable** feeling and use a specific word for how you felt. Avoid general words like happy, sad, angry, or mad. Be specific!

_____

_____

_____

_____

_____.

Write something that happened recently that gave you an **uncomfortable** feeling and use a specific word for how you felt. Avoid general words like happy, sad, angry, or mad. Be specific!

_____

_____

_____

_____

_____.

*It is **positive** to communicate with others when problems occur.* When you have a problem, it might be due to 1) an accident, 2) something that just happened because of the circumstances or a change in circumstances, or 3) a mistake that you or someone else made. None of those kinds of problems were done by someone on purpose to hurt or bother you, and it is positive for your reputation to be forgiving and helpful.

1. If you are the one having the problem, what should you say to others about it? Pick two for each problem!

   When there is an accident (no one expected it, it was a surprise):

   ❑ "That's okay, it was just an accident!"

   ❑ "You did that on purpose!"

   ❑ "No problem, it's fine."

   When something "just happens" (normal circumstances or a change in circumstances):

   ❑ "Oh well, these things just happen!"

   ❑ "It's not a big deal."

   ❑ "I'm not doing it."

   When you cause a problem because you made a mistake:

   ❑ "Whoops! I'm sorry!"

   ❑ "What can I do to help fix this?"

   ❑ "It's not my fault!"

2. If someone else is having the problem, it is positive to:

   ❑ Show you understand and care how they are feeling (uncomfortable!).

   ❑ Try to help.

   When you do these two things, people feel respected and valued, and they want to work with you or be your friend.

   Check the positive response to these problems that others are having:

   Someone can't find what they are looking for in the store where you work:

   ❑ "I'm sorry you can't find what you want, I will help you look."

   ❑ "I don't know where it is, either."

   Someone got extra work to do and they are worried they won't finish before the end of the day.

   ❑ "I'm done with mine."

   ❑ "I'm sure you feel overwhelmed. Do you want me to try to help you get it done?"

*It is **positive** to express confidence and pride in your work.* Employers want people who have self-confidence and a sense of pride in their work. It is positive to express this at work. If you don't feel comfortable being positive about yourself yet, go ahead and say positive things until you *do* feel comfortable. Sometimes you just have to practice!

Look in the mirror and practice saying aloud each of the following sentences, just as you might say them at work. ***Make sure that your voice and your face are upbeat and friendly.*** Then check the boxes to show that you said them positively.

"I'm really learning a lot at this job!"   ☐ I *sounded* positive   ☐ I *looked* positive

"I think I can do it by myself now."   ☐ I *sounded* positive   ☐ I *looked* positive

"I will do that better next time."   ☐ I *sounded* positive   ☐ I *looked* positive

"I really like this job!"   ☐ I *sounded* positive   ☐ I *looked* positive

"I'm sure I can do it with some practice."   ☐ I *sounded* positive   ☐ I *looked* positive

"I will do it right next time."   ☐ I *sounded* positive   ☐ I *looked* positive

"I'm pretty good at this!"   ☐ I *sounded* positive   ☐ I *looked* positive

"Sure, I don't mind new things!"   ☐ I *sounded* positive   ☐ I *looked* positive

"This is my favorite part of the job."   ☐ I *sounded* positive   ☐ I *looked* positive

"Can you show me how to do it?"   ☐ I *sounded* positive   ☐ I *looked* positive

"I got that really clean!"   ☐ I *sounded* positive   ☐ I *looked* positive

*It is **positive** to say things that show that you accept others just as they are.* You meet many people through work, and everyone is very different. They have different opinions and preferences, different abilities, and sometimes disabilities, too. People aren't perfect! Everyone wants to be accepted and feel comfortable at work.

Your body language, including your face and voice tone, must be positive and friendly, even when your boss and coworkers aren't "perfect."

Look in the mirror and practice saying aloud each of the following sentences, just as you might say them at work. ***Make sure that your voice and your face are upbeat and friendly.*** Then check the boxes to show that you said them positively.

"No problem!"   ❑ I *sounded* positive   ❑ I *looked* positive

"It's totally okay!"   ❑ I *sounded* positive   ❑ I *looked* positive

"No worries."   ❑ I *sounded* positive   ❑ I *looked* positive

"Let me know if I can help!" ❑ I *sounded* positive   ❑ I *looked* positive

"Keep trying, you'll get it!" ❑ I *sounded* positive   ❑ I *looked* positive

"It's not a big deal."   ❑ I *sounded* positive   ❑ I *looked* positive

"I don't mind!"   ❑ I *sounded* positive   ❑ I *looked* positive

"You're a big help to me."   ❑ I *sounded* positive   ❑ I *looked* positive

"Nobody's perfect!"   ❑ I *sounded* positive   ❑ I *looked* positive

*It is **positive** to speak in different ways with different people:* more relaxed with friends, more formally and respectfully with bosses.

Which of the following five sentences are **not** positive, appropriate ways to speak to your boss?

- ❑ "Yo, Mr. Martin!"

- ❑ "Mr. Martin, can I speak privately with you, please?"

- ❑ "Mr. Martin, I need your help with something."

- ❑ "I wonder if I can talk to you for a few minutes, Mr. Martin?"

- ❑ "Hey! Help me out here!"

Answer: *The first and last sentences are not positive because they are not appropriately formal and respectful for speaking with a boss.*

Try these pairs of sentences:

- ❑ "Okay, I'm done. I'm going to go rest now."
- ❑ "Mr. Martin, can you please check to see if I did everything you wanted?"

- ❑ "I'm going to go get the hose now."
- ❑ "Would you like me to go and get the hose now?"

- ❑ "Dude, this is ridiculous!"
- ❑ "Mr. Martin, I think I might need extra time to do all of this."

For each pair of sentences, which one is positive to say to a boss?

Answer: *For each pair, it is the second sentence that is positive and appropriate. You should frame your sentence as a **question** to ask the boss, not to tell him or her. It is more respectful to ask than to tell.*

It is **positive** to acknowledge and respond to others **every time** they speak to you or you start to speak to them. This makes people feel respected and valued. Look at the following examples and pick the one that acknowledges and responds to others best.

- Someone waves to you and says hello.
    - ❑ You wave back and say hello.
    - ❑ You turn and look away and say nothing.

- You are asked a question that you don't know the answer to.
    - ❑ You say "I don't know."
    - ❑ You say nothing and stare ahead of you.

- Someone bumps into you and says "excuse me."
    - ❑ You say "that's okay."
    - ❑ You say nothing and look away.

- Someone says "welcome!" when you walk into the room.
    - ❑ You say "thank you" and smile at them.
    - ❑ You ignore them and sit down.

- You have to get prescriptions filled. When you come up to the pharmacy window, the woman says "hello."
    - ❑ You say, "Hi, how are you today?" and wait for a response. Then you hand her the prescriptions to fill.
    - ❑ Hand her the prescriptions and say, "I need to get these filled."

- You want to have a conversation with your co-worker at lunch time. You wonder if he likes *StarCraft*, too.
    - ❑ You say, "Hi, how was work this morning?" and wait for an answer. Then you say, "Hey, do you like *StarCraft*?"
    - ❑ You immediately say, "Do you like *StarCraft*?"

Answers: For each of the above pairs, the first one acknowledges others best!

BODY LANGUAGE/ VOICE AND POSITIVITY:

BODY POSTURE/ ORIENTATION, FACIAL EXPRESSION, VOICE TONE AND VOLUME

Communicating positively at work is not limited to the words you say. You also communicate with your body, your face, and your voice. This is called "body language." Your body language must be positive to match your words!

This section has twenty ways to practice positive steps toward independence and employment if you struggle to read the body language of others or if you struggle to have body language that:

- Shows interest in others
- Shows respect for others
- Looks friendly
- Looks confident
- "Blends in" with others
- Acknowledges and greets others appropriately
- Shows patience while waiting
- Is not distracting to others
- Shows control (i.e., is neutral/positive) when you are upset
- Includes positive voice tone and volume
- Is positive in conversation
- Does not invade the personal space of others

*It is **positive** to have a friendly look on your face at all times, unless you are having a particular moment that is negative or uncomfortable for you.* You don't need to look "happy" all the time, but you should look friendly and approachable almost all of the time. If your face is friendly and approachable, then people will be comfortable around you and communicating with you, including your boss and co-workers.

1. During a period of some hours, "freeze" your face and go by a mirror to see what your expression is. Check the box that shows how your face looks, on average.

   My face is pleasant, friendly, and approachable ...

   ❑ All the time

   ❑ Some of the time (a few frowns)

   ❑ Not very often (usually frowning or severe looking)

   ❑ Never (always frowning and severe looking)

2. Ask at least one person that you trust to tell you if your face is pleasant, friendly, and approachable ...

   ❑ All the time

   ❑ Some of the time (a few frowns)

   ❑ Not very often (usually frowning or severe looking)

   ❑ Never (always frowning and severe looking)

If you checked the "not very often" or "never" boxes for 1 or 2 (or both) above, you need practice! Work at a more positive facial expression as often as you can think about it during the day (check in the mirror and ask your trusted person), and try to move up to the next level/box above where you were first marked. The goal is a positive face almost all of the time. Facial expression is a habit that you can change! A positive face day in and day out will help you have more friends and will help build your good reputation at work!

*It is **positive** to make eye contact with others, at minimum.*

1. When they are talking to you.

2. When you are acknowledging them (i.e., when you first meet or greet them, or want to show interest in them or a problem they are having).

If eye contact is hard for you, at least do it in those situations. More eye contact is usually better (with the exception of staring).

Practice the following sentences in front of the mirror or with a trusted person. Make eye contact while you are saying these things, and check the boxes to show you did it.

❑ "Hi, it's nice to meet you!"

❑ "How was your weekend? What did you do?" (Continue looking at the person while they answer this.)

❑ "Mr. Martin, what do you want me to do next?" (Continue looking at the person while they answer this.)

❑ "Thank you for helping me."

❑ "Wow, that's really tough. I'm sorry that happened to you."

❑ "Is there anything I can do to help you?" (Continue looking at the person while they answer this.)

❑ "What would you like me to do here?" (Continue looking at the person while they answer this.)

❑ "Welcome to our project!"

❑ "Wow, that must have hurt!"

❑ "Where do you want to start?"

❑ "Are you going to be working with us?"

❑ "When do I receive my first paycheck?"

*It is **positive** to turn your body to face someone who is talking, and/or who is in charge (i.e., your boss or supervisor).* Your body should be completely facing them with your shoulders turned toward them, even if you have to move to stand in another spot or turn your chair around. It shows respect and will increase your reputation.

Practice the previous sentences again, in front of a mirror or with a trusted person. This time, use eye contact **and** make sure that your body is completely facing the person you are speaking with.

- ❑ "Hi, it's nice to meet you!"

- ❑ "How was your weekend? What did you do?" (Continue looking at the person while they answer this.)

- ❑ "Mr. Martin, what do you want me to do next?" (Continue looking at the person while they answer this.)

- ❑ "Thank you for helping me."

- ❑ "Wow, that's really tough. I'm sorry that happened to you."

- ❑ "Is there anything I can do to help you?" (Continue looking at the person while they answer this.)

- ❑ "What would you like me to do here?" (Continue looking at the person while they answer this.)

- ❑ "Welcome to our project!"

- ❑ "Wow, that must have hurt!"

- ❑ "Where do you want to start?"

- ❑ "Are you going to be working with us?"

- ❑ "When do I receive my first paycheck?"

*It is **positive** to keep your body in its own space—that includes your arms, legs, and even your voice.* Your voice should usually fill the space just around you, and not go into the "hearing space" of others at a distance (e.g., across the room). You can go into the space of family members and close friends more, but usually you should be about an arm's length away from others when talking. When you stay in your own space, it makes everyone feel more comfortable.

Practice the following and check the boxes when you have done it.

❑ Talk to someone while you are **standing** for at least five minutes and keep your body and voice in your own space.

❑ Talk to someone while you are **sitting** for at least five minutes and keep your body and voice in your own space.

❑ Talk to someone while you are both **walking** for at least five minutes and keep your body and voice in your own space.

❑ Talk to someone while you are both **standing outside** for at least five minutes and keep your body and voice in your own space.

*It is **positive** to keep your body quiet when you are around others: your arms, legs, and head should be still, and your mouth quiet unless it is your turn to talk.* When your body is moving, it distracts others and might look disrespectful, like you're uninterested in your work, and does not "blend in" with your coworkers.

If you feel you must move your arms and legs at work, what are some positive things that you can do? Check the appropriate things you can do while on the job.

> ❑ Ask to take a break and go for a walk.
>
> ❑ Wave your arms over your head a few times.
>
> ❑ Jump up and down right where you are.
>
> ❑ Ask to take a break and go to a private place where you can stretch or move around for a bit.
>
> ❑ Move your head around in a circle ten times.

The correct answers are: 1 and 4. The other moves are distracting to others and do not "blend in" with your coworkers.

*It is **positive** to keep your body patient and still until it is your turn.* It is natural to be impatient while you wait for something you want, but you should try to not show this by keeping a neutral expression and a patient body. "Butting in" and excess movement while you wait are not positive and will decrease your reputation. Patient body language and waiting your turn calmly will increase it.

Imagine waiting in line for something you really want! Maybe you want to contribute to the conversation about something you are interested in with a group of people talking together, or maybe you are waiting to find out if you got the job assignment that you were wanting. "On the inside" you are excited or anxious, and it's hard to wait! "On the outside," that is, for **your appearance**, describe below how you will keep your body, face, and voice so that you appear calm and patient.

Body: _____

_____

_____

_____

_____

Face: _____

_____

_____

_____

_____

Voice: _____

_____

_____

_____

_____

*It is **positive** to use a pleasant, friendly, and accepting voice tone when speaking with others.* If your voice tone is negative, it can change the words you are saying to mean the opposite! People notice your voice tone and feel respected and comfortable when it is pleasant, friendly, and accepting. A whiny, complaining, bossy, or angry voice tone is negative and may give you a bad reputation!

See what a difference voice tone can make! In the following sentences, the words are positive. But if you say it with a negative voice tone, it changes the meaning to negative. Try it!

"That's great." (Say it in a **disgusted** voice tone.)

"It's hard to do." (Say it in a **frustrated** voice tone.)

"That's what I said." (Say it in an **angry** voice tone.)

"I want that one!" (Say it in a **whiny** voice tone.)

Now say the above sentences with a positive voice tone. Try it with a trusted person.

Did they hear the difference?   YES / NO

Did you hear the difference?   YES / NO

*It is **positive** to use an appropriate voice volume for where you are, what you are doing, and how close others are to you.* Your boss and coworkers will feel that you are considerate and respectful if you always use an appropriate voice volume, and this is good for your reputation.

Voice volume scale: 0 - Silence, 1 - Whisper, 2 - Inside Voice, 3 - Outside Voice, 4 - Yelling

Circle the appropriate response for each situation.

A. For your job at the park, you need to use the hose. You see someone at some distance from you near the hose and you want them to bring it. There are no park visitors nearby and no one is standing near you. What do you do? Check the correct answer(s).

- ❏ 1. Wave silently and hope the person near the hose sees you.
- ❏ 2. Walk over to the person near the hose to tell them you need it.
- ❏ 3. Go get the hose yourself.
- ❏ 4. Call out at a "3" or "4" to "please bring the hose!"

B. For your job at the park, you need to use the hose. You see someone at some distance from you near the hose and you want them to bring it. There are no park visitors nearby, but a coworker is standing near you. What do you do? Check the correct answer(s).

- ❏ 1. Wave silently and hope the person sees you.
- ❏ 2. Walk over to the person near the hose.
- ❏ 3. Go get the hose yourself.
- ❏ 4. Call out at a "3" or "4" to "please bring the hose!"

C. For your job at the park, you need to use the hose. You see someone at some distance from you near the hose and you want them to bring it. There are park visitors nearby. What do you do? Check the correct answer(s).

- ❏ 1. Wave silently and hope the person sees you.
- ❏ 2. Walk over to the person near the hose.
- ❏ 3. Go get the hose yourself.
- ❏ 4. Call out at a "3" or "4" to "please bring the hose!"

Answers: *A) All are okay   B) 1, 2, 3 only are okay   C) 1, 2, 3 are only okay*

*It is **positive** to greet others every time it is expected.* It does not matter if you know the person or if the person is a stranger. It is expected that you will greet others if:

1. They greet you first (you can accomplish this by waving, nodding, or saying hello).

2. You already greeted them once, but you were separated (they left your area or you left theirs) and then you pass each other or are in the same area together again.

It makes others feel noticed when you greet them, so it is respectful. It will increase your reputation if you greet others every time it is expected.

Mark the boxes for when you should greet someone.

❑ Someone waves at you from far away.

❑ Someone you greeted earlier left your room and then later passes you in a hallway.

❑ Someone comes into the room where you are standing.

❑ Someone you greeted earlier comes back into the room where you are.

❑ Someone says hello to you first.

❑ You are introduced to someone by someone else.

❑ Someone shakes your hand.

***Correct Answers:** All of the above!*

Mark all the appropriate ways that you can greet someone:

❑ "Hello!"

❑ "Hello again." (If you saw them earlier.)

❑ "Hi, nice to see you."

❑ "How do you do?"

❑ "Glad to meet you."

❑ (Waving to someone.)

❑ (Nodding at someone.)

***Correct Answers:** All of the above!*

*It is **positive** to always **acknowledge** others and to respond to them.*

*It is **positive** to always **respond** to others, even if you are not sure what to say.*

Acknowledging:

This means that you notice them, and it shows them that you feel they are important. This is respectful. If you see someone, you should acknowledge them by making eye contact, smiling, and/or nodding and/or saying hello. Acknowledging is the first thing you do with **anyone**. Even if you have business with them (e.g., you are filling a prescription, buying groceries, getting your oil changed), you must first acknowledge the other person before you talk about the business you are doing with them. Which of the following is acknowledging others?

1. Saying hello.
2. Just making eye contact with the person and smiling.
3. "Hi, how are you?"
4. Turning your body to face someone, smiling, and nodding.
5. "Here, I need you to look at this."
6. "How much does it cost?"
7. Continuing to work at the computer when your boss comes into the room.

***Correct Answers:** 1, 2, 3, 4*

Responding:

Responding is a special kind of acknowledging, where someone says something to you and you are expected to say something back. The thing they say to you might be a question and you are expected to give an answer. You must always respond, as it helps people to feel respected and comfortable around you. If you do not respond, they might feel you do not like them, or that you are rude or not nice. If you do not know how to respond, or what to say, you simply say so! For example, "I don't know," "I don't know how to answer that," "I don't know the answer," "I'm not sure what we are talking about," "I'm confused, can you straighten me out?" It is fine to not know what to say back, but you must say something whenever someone speaks to you and waits for an answer. Your body language needs to be friendly and accepting.

Circle the acceptable responses when someone speaks to you or asks you a question.

1. "I don't know."
2. "Can you explain that to me?"
3. "I'm confused about that."
4. "I need more information."
5. "I can get someone to answer your question."
6. Staring at the person and not answering.
7. Looking away silently.

***Correct Answers:** 1, 2, 3, 4, 5*

*It is **positive** to acknowledge someone before you start to make conversation with them.* How do you acknowledge another person? There are a few things you must do: you first turn your body to face them, have a pleasant facial expression, make eye contact, and greet them ("Hello, how are you doing?" "It's good to see you," "What's up?"). When you acknowledge someone before you start a conversation with them, you are showing respect and interest in them.

Pretend you **just walked up to someone** and say the following. Which of the following is okay? Circle "yes" if it is okay (acknowledges the person), and "no" if it is not okay (does not acknowledge the person).

A. Pleasant face, facing person, eye contact: "Hi, how's it going? (Wait for a response.) "Guess what happened to me last night?"   YES / NO

B. Pleasant face, facing person, eye contact: "I had a really weird dream last night where I was an astronaut and ..."   YES / NO

C. Pleasant face, facing person, eye contact: "Hey there, what's up?" (Wait for a response.) "I'm going to visit my dad this weekend, I love baseball so we are going to a baseball game ..."   YES / NO

D. Pleasant face, facing person, eye contact: "I'm going to visit my dad this weekend, I love baseball so we are going to a baseball game ..."   YES / NO

E. Pleasant face, facing person, eye contact: "I haven't seen you for a really long time! How are things going?" (Wait for a response.) "Things have sure changed in our town. They are building new apartments where our school used to be ..."   YES / NO

F. Pleasant face, facing person, eye contact: "Things have sure changed in our town. They are building new apartments where our school used to be ..."   YES / NO

G. Looking away, face looks negative/not friendly: "I started here last week and I've been doing inventory, but I put in for a change. Do you like inventory?"   YES / NO

H. Looking away, face looks negative/not friendly: "Hey, guess what? I started here last week and I've been doing inventory, but I put in for a change. Do you like inventory?"
                                                                                                                                 YES / NO

I. Eye contact, friendly face: "Hi, how's it going? (Wait for a response.) "I started here last week and I've been doing inventory, but I put in for a change. Do you like inventory?"
                                                                                                                                 YES / NO

Answers: *"Yes": A, C, E, I*

*It is **positive** to show interest in others.* You show interest with your body and face and voice tone. When you show interest, others feel respected and it increases your reputation.

How it looks:

Body: Facing the person who is speaking, nodding while you are listening.

Face: Friendly and interested, respectful, eye contact while you are listening.

How it sounds:

Voice tone is pleasant, neutral, or positive; voice is not whining, complaining, negative.

Pretend someone is telling you something. Say the following sentences in front of a mirror or a trusted person, looking and sounding interested. Check the boxes when you do it.

"Wow!"	❑ I *sounded* positive	❑ I *looked* positive
"I can't believe that happened to you!"	❑ I *sounded* positive	❑ I *looked* positive
"That's amazing."	❑ I *sounded* positive	❑ I *looked* positive
"That's pretty interesting."	❑ I *sounded* positive	❑ I *looked* positive
"That is a surprise!"	❑ I *sounded* positive	❑ I *looked* positive
"I would never have guessed that."	❑ I *sounded* positive	❑ I *looked* positive
"I've never heard that before."	❑ I *sounded* positive	❑ I *looked* positive
"I will see what I can do for you."	❑ I *sounded* positive	❑ I *looked* positive
"That's a good deal."	❑ I *sounded* positive	❑ I *looked* positive

It is **positive** to show interest in others, **even when you are not interested!** You show interest with your body and face and voice tone. It is not easy to show interest when you are really not interested, but it is very important! When you show interest (even when you don't feel it), then others feel respected and it increases your reputation. If you do not show interest, the other person will very likely feel offended and may think you are a rude person. This is especially a big issue when listening to your boss, someone you want to hire you or work with you, or any authority figure.

Your interest in what someone is saying does not need to be sincere; your sincere interest in the person feeling respected and valued is what is important.

Circle the numbers for good ways to show interest (even when you are not interested).

1. Nod your head while making eye contact

2. Blurt something out while they are speaking.

3. Change the subject.

4. Make eye contact.

5. Turn your body toward the person speaking.

6. Don't talk to others while that person is speaking.

7. Look away.

8. Ask a question about what they are saying.

9. Don't interrupt the person who is speaking.

10. Take notes.

Correct Answers: 1, 4, 5, 6, 8, 9, 10

*It is **positive** to show self-confidence, interest in others, respect for others, and interest in what you are doing through your body posture.* Slumping over, curling up, drawing your legs up in front of you while you are sitting, turning your body away from people, putting your head down, and putting your head in your arms all indicate to others that you are not confident in yourself and/ or not interested in them and/or disrespectful.* Employers want to hire confident people who show interest in their work and in others, and workers and friends want to be with those who show interest in them and are positive and respectful.

Talk with a trusted person who knows you well. Which body postures have they noticed that you need to be aware of and avoid when you are with others?

❑ Slumping over

❑ Curling up

❑ Drawing your legs up in front of you while you are sitting

❑ Turning your body away from people

❑ Putting your head down

❑ Putting your head in your arms

❑ Other:_____

❑ No negative body postures

---

* You may feel respectful, confident, and interested, but others may believe you are not if they observe the body postures listed above.

*It is **positive** to maintain neutral or positive body language when you are upset or having problems at work.* Even if you have strong negative feelings and you are upset, you need to continue to try to focus on your work and to not let it show very much. You should consider the type of problem you are having and say and do something appropriate to solve your problem and/or cope with it, instead of showing negativity with your body language. Other people notice you and read your body language, and they will feel comfortable working with you if you handle problems with patience and self-control. Your boss and coworkers will think you are dependable and mature, and this will increase your reputation!

Which of the following are **not** neutral or positive body language?

1. Shouting in an angry voice.

2. Maintaining a friendly face.

3. Clenching your fists.

4. Stomping your feet.

5. Using a quiet voice to speak to your coworkers.

6. Using a quiet and calm voice tone to ask for a break.

7. Making a "mad face" at someone.

Correct answers are: 1, 3, 4, 7

*It is **positive** for your body language (face/body/voice) to blend in with others around you.* If you match what others look like in your posture, your movements, your facial expression, and your voice tone and volume, then you are "blending." This makes you more a part of the group and people will feel comfortable being around you.

Consider the following situations. Please circle "yes" if it is blending and "no" if it is not blending.

A. You are working with a group of people and you make little noises from time to time (no one else is making noises). YES / NO

B. You are sitting for a long time with others and you lie on the floor to stretch out for a few minutes (everyone else stays seated). YES / NO

C. Everyone is standing together listening to your boss and you are standing with them listening, too. YES / NO

D. Everyone is sweeping, and you are using your broom like a guitar. YES / NO

E. Everyone is looking at their computers and working, and you are, too. YES / NO

Answers: *"Yes" for blending are C and E*

*It is **positive** to read the body language of others, so that you know if they are interested in what you are saying or doing.* If others are not interested, then you should stop what you are doing or saying and move on. Everyone has different interests, preferences, and things they are thinking about; if they are not interested right now, that does not mean anything negative about you. And they might be interested later! Be positive if you see "not interested" body language, and move on!

Describe what "not interested" body language looks like below. Check with a trusted person to see if you have it right.

Consider the statements below for "not interested" body language. Mark the ones that may indicate someone is "not interested."

- ❑ 1) Looks away
- ❑ 2) Changes the subject
- ❑ 3) Makes eye contact, nods head while you are talking
- ❑ 4) Leaves you and does something else
- ❑ 5) Moves closer to you
- ❑ 6) Moves farther from you
- ❑ 7) Says, "I'm not interested in that"
- ❑ 8) Says something back on your topic

Answers: 1, 2, 4, 6, 7

Now consider the statements below for "interested" body language. Mark the ones that may indicate someone is "interested."

- ❑ 1) Looks away
- ❑ 2) Changes the subject
- ❑ 3) Makes eye contact, nods head while you are talking
- ❑ 4) Leaves you and does something else
- ❑ 5) Moves closer to you
- ❑ 6) Moves farther from you
- ❑ 7) Says, "I'm not interested in that"
- ❑ 8) Says something back on your topic

Answers: 3, 5, 8

*It is **positive** to read the body language of others, so that you know if they are feeling **comfortable**.* Comfortable body language might mean that they are "having a good day" and not experiencing problems at work or in their life, and it might also mean that they are comfortable being with you! If they are with you and are showing "comfortable" body language, they are comfortable with the topic you are talking about and/or the things you are doing. That is good to know!

Which of the following may show that someone is feeling "comfortable?"

1. Moving around a lot in their seat or while standing.

2. Looking around and not making eye contact.

3. Smiling and leaning back, looking relaxed.

4. Not "in a hurry": calm and relaxed body.

5. Looking away and saying, "Sorry, I can't stay; I have things to do."

6. Greeting you, smiling, and starting a conversation or adding to the conversation.

Answers: *3, 4, and 6*

*It is **positive** to read the body language of others, so that you know if they are feeling **uncomfortable**.* Uncomfortable body language might mean that they are "having a bad day" and experiencing problems at work or in their life. It could also be an indication that they are uncomfortable with the topic you are talking about, and/or the things you are doing. Usually people won't tell you they are uncomfortable, you have to read their body language. It is important to know so you can adjust what you are saying or doing. When people are comfortable around you, that builds both friendships and your reputation.

Which of the following may show that someone is feeling "uncomfortable?"

1. Moving around a lot in their seat or while standing.

2. Looking around and not making eye contact.

3. Smiling and leaning back, looking relaxed.

4. Not "in a hurry": calm and relaxed body.

5. Looking away and saying, "Sorry, I can't stay; I have things to do."

6. Greeting you, smiling, and starting a conversation or adding to the conversation.

Answers: 1, 2, 5

It is **positive** to have confident body language, including your head, eyes, face, posture, and actions, when you interact with others. Customers, co-workers, and employers know they can depend on you and are more comfortable being around you when you project confidence with your body.

Even if you are **not** confident, you should try to look as if you are! This is not being "insincere" or "fake," it is a sincere effort to blend in, make others comfortable, and practice an important skill!

Which are body language behaviors that look confident?

1. Eye contact with someone.

2. Shaking hands and saying "hello."

3. Standing at a distance from someone.

4. Walking up to someone and greeting them.

5. Standing in the corner of a room by yourself.

6. Turning away from others while sitting in your chair.

7. Head up.

8. Head down.

9. Walking up to someone, making eye contact, then asking for help with something.

10. Pushing your chair away from the table where others are sitting.

11. Facing people you are talking to.

Answers: 1, 2, 4, 7, 9, 11

INTENSITY AND POSITIVITY:

STRONG FEELINGS/

PREFERENCES/OPINIONS

Your strong feelings, preferences, and opinions can be good—it is a sign that you care and are engaged in your life! However, great intensity in these areas can sometimes be a barrier to success on the job and in relationships with others. *It is **positive** to recognize and manage the intensity of your feelings, preferences, and opinions so that you can be successful.* Are you someone who ...

• Gets angry/frustrated when you can't do your desired or preferred activities?

• Becomes upset when you have to do something that you don't prefer to do?

• Avoids or refuses new activities, or learning/participating in new things because they are not your favorite things to do or you are very anxious about them?

• Has strong negative opinions about topics and/or individuals?

This section has twenty ways to practice positive steps toward independence and employment if you struggle with strong feelings, preferences, and opinions, in the following areas:

• Understanding and expressing what you are feeling.

• Recognizing how intense your feeling is.

• Understanding how other people may feel differently.

• Coping with intense feelings.

• "Scaling back" or limiting your intensity as appropriate.

• Recognizing intense opinions.

• Expressing intense feelings/preferences/opinions at the appropriate time, place, and with the appropriate person at work.

• Intensity and appropriate body language.

• Intensity and voice tone/volume.

• Intensity and the feelings/comfort of others.

• Intensity and "blending in."

• Limiting negative intensity (complaining, anger, frustration).

• Limiting positive intensity.

• Intensity and misinterpreting: responding positively to others and avoiding negative interpretations at work.

• Intensity and conflict.

• Intensity and working toward "middle ground" in opinions and feelings.

• Intensity and doing something you don't prefer to do.

• Intensity and not being able to do something you strongly prefer.

• Developing "backup" choices when your preference may be unavailable.

*It is **positive** to recognize which uncomfortable feelings you are experiencing intensely, so that you can express them appropriately to solve your problems.* When feelings are intensely "uncomfortable," for example when we are embarrassed, frustrated, anxious, or disappointed, we sometimes just express anger. It is not helpful in any setting, but particularly at work, to respond to a wide variety of uncomfortable feelings with anger.

Consider the following situations and mark the most positive way to deal with intense uncomfortable feelings.

- You got a job assignment that you have not done before.

    ❑ "Hi Mr. Martin, you put me on the schedule for closing the shop but I haven't done that before; I feel really **nervous** about it. Can I have a different job? Or can I get some practice before I have to do it?"

    ❑ "Hey! I am not closing the shop! That makes me really mad! Why did you put me on the schedule for that? I quit!"

- You asked to work with animals in the barn but someone else was chosen to do it this week.

    ❑ "I am really **disappointed** I wasn't picked to work with the animals. Will I have a chance next week? How can I show that I would be able to do it?"

    ❑ "What the heck! I really wanted to be in the barn, I've waited a long time, and you're not letting me do it! That's ridiculous, I'm better with the animals than everybody else!"

- You made a mistake twice by not turning off the machines at the end of the day.

    ❑ "I'm not going back to work. My boss is mean, and he is always criticizing me!"

    ❑ "I'm so **embarrassed** that I messed up twice on the same thing! I don't feel like going back to work because I am too **embarrassed**. What do you think I should do?"

- You keep miscounting the number of pieces in the container.

    ❑ "I'm so stupid! I can't get this right! This is a really dumb job and I hate it!"

    ❑ "I'm really **frustrated** right now. Can I take a break for five minutes?

*It is **positive** to recognize how intense your feelings are.* When you are feeling uncomfortable feelings at a "3" intensity (see scale below), you need to notice it right away so that you can do something to prevent them from becoming a "4."

Look at the scale below.

How Strong Are Your Uncomfortable Feelings?				
0	**1**	**2**	**3**	**4**
0 = Not at all	1 = A little	2 = Somewhat	3 = Quite a bit	4 = Very

List at least two ways you will notice when you are feeling uncomfortable at a level "3" (these might include pacing, voice gets louder, feeling more anxious, wanting to be left alone, etc.). They will be different for everyone. Ask someone who knows you well if they can help you with what you should notice.

1. _____

_____

_____

_____

_____.

2. _____

_____

_____

_____

_____.

*It is **positive** to "dial it back" or cope if you are feeling uncomfortable feelings at a "3" intensity (see scale below), before they become a "4."* You can cope in ways that work for you (suggestions below) to "dial it back." It is much harder to dial back your feelings and manage your emotions and behaviors when you are already at a "4." You should try very hard to not reach a "4," especially in a work setting. When you can manage your strong feelings at work, that increases your reputation and people know they can depend on you.

Look at the scale below. When you are feeling uncomfortable at a 3 or 4 level, you may need to have **positive** ways to cope or deal with those uncomfortable feelings.

How Strong Are Your Uncomfortable Feelings?				
0	**1**	**2**	**3**	**4**
0 = Not at all	1 = A little	2 = Somewhat	3 = Quite a bit	4 = Very

*It is **positive** to "dial back" your intense feelings by:*

• Speaking to someone about it

• Taking a walk

• Playing with your pet

• Writing it down

• Reading a book

• Listening to music

There are many ways that people deal with their uncomfortable intense feelings so they can "dial it back!" Write down two **positive** ways that you can cope when you feel "quite a bit" uncomfortable ("3"), so you don't become "very" uncomfortable ("4"):

_____

_____

_____.

It is positive to check if your feelings intensity matches the problem level. Problems create uncomfortable feelings, and anxiety might increase those feelings so that they become more intense. This might happen even if the problem is not what most people would consider a very big problem! When you are having intense, uncomfortable feelings related to a problem, consider the problem level scale below.

Problem Level Scale

1. Slight problem (might need/want to fix it, possibly a bit uncomfortable)
2. Minor problem (inconvenient, somewhat uncomfortable)
3. Significant problem (quite uncomfortable and requires solution)
4. Major problem (emergency, cannot be fixed, catastrophic)

Next, consider an intensity scale for how intense your uncomfortable feeling related to your problem is:

Uncomfortable Feeling Intensity Scale				
0	**1**	**2**	**3**	**4**
0 = Not at all	1 = A little	2 = Somewhat	3 = Quite a bit	4 = Very

Does your feeling intensity match the level of problem you are having? Although people might vary in how serious they think any problem is, many people will agree on problems that are very small or very big. If you lose your favorite pencil, most people would call that only a very slight problem (a "1"). If you feel a "3" or "4" for intensity for any problem:

1. Identify the level of the problem you have (check with others you can trust!).
2. Check if your intensity of feeling matches the level of your problem.*

---

* If you are feeling more intense than your problem, you need to "cope" so you can scale back those uncomfortable feelings. Here are some ways to cope. Write two more ways to cope in the blanks provided:

Positive self-talk ("It will be okay," "It's not that bad," etc.)
Take a break
Speak to someone about it
Take a walk
Write it down
Listen to music

_____

_____

*It is **positive** to recognize that other people may feel less strongly than you do about the same things.* Everyone is different in the intensity of their feelings, and also in what they judge to be a significant problem. Please consider that if your intensity of feeling is a lot more than most people would feel about the same thing, your coworkers and your boss might judge your intensity to be inappropriate. That is not good for your reputation. So, you need to consider how others might respond less strongly to the things that feel very intense to you and go for "dialing it back" or working toward feeling more neutral and calm—or at least appearing so when you are at work! That is positive and good for your reputation.

List at least two things that make you feel uncomfortable at a "3" or a "4," i.e., "quite a bit" or "very" uncomfortable. These can be things such as making mistakes, being told to do something over, having to make a sudden and unexpected change, not getting to do your favorite thing, etc. Then ask someone you know and trust what number they are for those same things. If they are at a 0, 1, or 2 for their feelings about those things, will they think you are inappropriate at a "4?" Remember that at work, your reputation depends on always being appropriate.

How Strong Are Your Uncomfortable Feelings?

0	1	2	3	4
0 = Not at all	1 = A little	2 = Somewhat	3 = Quite a bit	4 = Very

Things that make me feel uncomfortable at a "3" or "4":

_____

_____

How _____ feels about those same things:

_____

_____

If I showed intense feelings about those things at work, would that look inappropriate to others?   YES / NO

What does your partner think?   YES / NO

*It is **positive** to be aware of your intense opinions, and limit expressing them with others at work.* If you have strong opinions that a thing or person is the best or the worst, you need to be aware of it so that you can limit sharing or expressing those opinions in the workplace. Some topics are relatively benign: they are unlikely to offend others or make them uncomfortable. If you express strong opinions about weather ("I hate when it rains!"), coworkers and bosses will probably continue to be comfortable and not offended. Strong opinions on some topics might possibly offend others.

If you express intense opinions about video games, movies, TV programs, or restaurants, this could be a problem and would need to at least be limited to appropriate time, place, and person. For example, your strong opinion that *StarCraft* is the best game ever might be shared in a limited way, with another young co-worker who also loves *StarCraft* at lunch time.

It will certainly be a problem if you have strong opinions that you express at work in the area of politics, religion, divisive news issues such as abortion or immigration, or negative opinions about either well-known people or people at work. These strong opinions should not be expressed at work at any time.

Do you have a strong opinion on a topic that you think would **not** offend or make anyone uncomfortable? (Suggestion: Ask a trusted person to help you with this.)

_____

_____

_____

Do you have a strong opinion on a topic that you think **could** or **would** offend or make someone uncomfortable? (Suggestion: Ask a trusted person to help you with this.)

_____

_____

_____

Play it safe and do not express these opinions in the workplace!

*It is **positive** to have positive or neutral body language when you are sharing strong feelings or opinions.* Whether your intense feelings are positive (e.g., being in love or super excited) or negative (e.g., deeply frustrated or very embarrassed), you need to maintain positive body language. This is respectful to others and shows you are dependable, calm, and focused at work. That's good for your reputation!

Circle the numbers for the correct ways to have neutral or positive body language:

1. Jumping up and down

2. Head up

3. Straight posture

4. Grabbing your head with your hands

5. Calm arms, hands, and legs

6. Head down

7. Twisting and bending down and away from others

Answers: 2, 3, 5

*It is **positive** to have appropriate voice tone and volume when you are sharing strong feelings or opinions.* Whether your intense feelings are positive (e.g., being in love, or super excited) or negative (e.g., deeply frustrated, or very embarrassed), you need to maintain an appropriate voice tone and volume. This is respectful to others and shows you are dependable, calm, and focused at work. That's good for your reputation!

Circle the numbers for the correct ways to have appropriate voice tone and volume:

1. Yelling

2. Inside voice

3. Calm voice

4. Complaining voice

5. Whining

6. Respectful voice

Answers: 2, 3, 6

*It is **positive** to speak in a limited way, or not at all, when you are sharing strong feelings or opinions at work.* This is respectful to others and shows you are dependable, calm, and focused at work. That's good for your reputation!

A. If your intense feelings are positive (e.g., being in love, super excited about a trip, or you love your new video game) you need to make sure that your words are appropriate for the workplace, that is, are "limited" or are not expressed at all.

> "Limited talk": intense positive feelings at work must not contain negative comparisons ("*StarCraft* is amazing, *Zelda* is stupid"), not be personal ("You look so beautiful today."), not happen often, not be talked about at length, should only shared with appropriate person (someone sharing your intense positive feeling/opinion), and at appropriate time and place that is allowed by your boss (usually okay at break or at lunch, but may not be okay while working).

> "No talk" (i.e., *do not express!*): for intense positive feelings at work: when feel you are "love struck," or think someone is attractive.

B. If your intense feelings are negative or uncomfortable (embarrassed, frustrated, anxious, etc.), or your intense opinions might make others uncomfortable, then you need to make sure that your words are appropriate for the workplace, that is, are "limited" or are not expressed at all.

> "Limited talk": you express negative feelings/opinions respectfully at the right time/place with the right person at work *if it is necessary*, as in the case of speaking privately to your boss about harassment on the job. Uncomfortable feelings should of course be shared at home with family, trusted others outside of work, or with a therapist.

> "No talk" (i.e., *do not express!*): *if it is not necessary* to share them, play it safe and keep strong negative feelings and opinions to yourself at work, or ask a trusted person what you should say and to whom.

Give at least one reason why you should limit positive or negative talk in areas you have strong opinions and feelings:

_____

_____

_____

*It is **positive** to read the body language of others, so that you know if your intensity is making them uncomfortable.* You might think it is okay to express your strong feeling or opinion in a limited way, or you might be looking for someone who shares your feelings or opinions at work. However, they may be uncomfortable with the topic you are talking about, and/or what you are saying and how/when/where you are saying it! Often people won't tell you they are uncomfortable, you have to read their body language. It is important to know so you can adjust what you are saying and doing. If people are showing "uncomfortable" body language, you need to move from "limited talk" to "no talk." When people are always comfortable around you, that builds both friendships and your reputation at work.

Which of the following may show that someone is feeling "uncomfortable?"

1. Moving around a lot in their seat or while standing.

2. Looking around and not making eye contact.

3. Smiling and leaning back, looking relaxed.

4. Changing the subject.

5. Not "in a hurry": calm and relaxed body.

6. Looking away and saying, "Sorry, I can't stay; I have things to do."

7. Not responding to you.

8. Responding in a limited way.

9. Adding to the conversation.

10. Responding to your questions and comments with a smile and eye contact.

Answers: 1, 2, 4, 6, 7, 8

*It is **positive** to match the intensity of those around you.* When you are with others, look around and see what everyone else is doing, how they are behaving, and what they are saying. If you match with them or "blend in," you are probably okay. If you are much more intense than others in your actions, your body language, and your words, or you are "doing your own thing," you are probably not blending in. This could make others uncomfortable and may mean that you are not doing satisfactory work for your boss. If you are having a strong feeling or opinion that is negative, or even if it is positive, you may need to "dial it back" to match the intensity of the group you are with. When you blend in with others, your boss and coworkers will see you as a dependable member of their group, and this is positive for your reputation. Mark the situations that show "blending in" with others.

❑ 1) Everyone is working at their computers; you had some trouble with yours and banged your fist down hard on your computer, startling your coworkers and your boss.

❑ 2) Your whole group is cleaning out the pens for the animals at the zoo, and even though you really hate the job, you are doing it, too.

❑ 3) Your group is cleaning out a shed at work. You are very frustrated because the work is taking a long time and also anxious because you think you won't finish before 5:00 p.m. However, you focus on looking and sounding neutral or positive like everyone else and continue working like the others.

❑ 4) You are very excited because you get a new video game today that you've been wanting a long time; your coworkers are pulling weeds at the park, but you are mostly talking about how cool the game is.

❑ 5) You have to be at the bakery by 5:30 a.m. Your coworkers get there on time; however, you hate getting up in the morning and you are refusing to do it, making you late most days.

❑ 6) You are cleaning vacated apartments and your boss wants you to clean even places that no one can see. You feel strongly that this is stupid and you complain about it, saying it's pointless. Your coworkers are just following the directions of the boss and not complaining.

❑ 7) Your coworkers are celebrating someone's birthday at lunch. You are very uncomfortable being with the group for that, but you show up, smile, and sing "Happy Birthday" with everyone else.

Answer: 2, 3, 7 are examples of "blending in" despite strong feelings and opinions.

*It is **positive** to understand how both positive intensity and negative intensity can be issues at work.* Whether your intense feelings are positive (e.g., "love-struck" or super excited,) or negative (e.g., deeply frustrated or very embarrassed), the workplace is seldom a good place to express those feelings. Pick one of the consequences of expressing your positive or negative intensity at work, and describe how that could happen.

❑ People may think you are not dependable or stable in your thinking and/or behavior.

❑ Coworkers may feel uncomfortable around you.

❑ Bosses may feel that you are spending more time talking (or complaining) than working.

❑ Bosses and coworkers may feel you are distracting them from their work.

❑ People may get their feelings hurt.

Describe/explain how that consequence could happen. Ask a trusted person to help you with this.

_____

_____

_____

_____

_____

*It is **positive** to limit expressing negative intensity to a "2" or less on the intensity scale, no matter how uncomfortable you are feeling in the workplace.*

Negative Intensity Scale

1. No negative body language/word choices.
2. Possible slight negative body language/word choices.
3. Some negative body language/word choices.
4. Significant negative body language/word choice (i.e., "acting out" physically, swearing/insulting/refusing/etc).

In general, responding to problems with negative intensity above a level "2" is inappropriate at work, and may cause you to lose your job. Although people at work do complain occasionally and feel angry or frustrated sometimes, long-term successful employees hold their negative intensity to no more than a "2," no matter how uncomfortable they are feeling. When you limit expressing negative intensity at work, other employees and your boss will feel comfortable around you and will feel that you are dependable. This is great for your reputation!

To limit expressing intense negative feelings above a level "2," you may:

1. Consider your level of problem and apply some coping methods to "dial back" your intensity of feeling, following the suggestions in #83.
2. "Pretend" you are calmer and less intense than you really feel! It is not wrong or bad to limit your intensity in this way; making others comfortable and keeping your job and your reputation are the most important things. Creating calm body language and positive word choices that do not actually match your negative intensity is **positive**.
3. Limit talking to others about your problem in the workplace.

Tell what you will do with your body ("body language") and what you will say to show calmness and positivity when you are feeling intensely negative at work:

Body languge: _____

Word choices: _____

*It is **positive** to limit expressing your positive intensity to a "2" or less on the intensity scale, no matter how happy/excited/lovestruck/enthusiastic you are feeling in the workplace.*

Positive Intensity Scale

1. A few limited positive body language/word choices (thumbs up or ok gesture/smile/"I'm excited!," "Wow," "Cool!").
2. Some/occasional positive body language/word choices (same as "1" but slightly more frequent or lengthy).
3. Frequent positive body language/word choices (lots of talking about reason for positive intensity, increased physical activity that is not work related, has to be asked to stop talking or refocus activity).
4. Dominating and ongoing positive body language/word choice (high intensity and frequency of physical activity that is not work related, talking repeatedly and at length about focus of positive intensity and will not stop when asked to do so).

In general, expressing a positive intensity above a level "2" is inappropriate at work, and may cause you to lose your job. Although people at work do "celebrate" and talk about areas of interest and pleasure sometimes, long-term successful employees do not have to be asked to refocus their activity or to stop talking about the focus of their positive intensity (level "2"). If that happens to you, dial it back! If you hold your positive intensity to no more than a "2" in the workplace, other employees and your boss will feel comfortable around you, and will feel that you are dependable. This is great for your reputation!

Expressing sexual attraction to someone or making personal comments about someone's appearance, even with positive intensity, are not appropriate in the workplace.

Tell what you will do with your body ("body language") and what you will say to limit your positive intensity at work. Think about how often you talk about something and how much you are focused on your work.

Body languge: _____

Word choices: _____

*It is **positive** to limit expressing intensity in the workplace, so that you may avoid expressing positive or negative intensity inappropriately.* It is challenging for everyone to interact without misunderstandings with coworkers and bosses; it is extra challenging for individuals on the autism spectrum. If you feel that someone said or did something on purpose to hurt or bother you, or if someone caused you to feel very uncomfortable, you may have an intensely **negative** feeling toward that person. If you feel that a coworker likes you romantically, you may have an intensely **positive** feeling toward that person! What if you misinterpreted the situations, the body language, and the words they used? Misunderstandings are another reason that it is important to limit expressing both positive and negative intensity in the workplace.

Check out the following work situations, and mark which responses are level "2" or lower based on the negative and positive intensity scales in #93 and #94, respectively.

- Someone borrowed your stapler and didn't put it back. Even though you were quite a bit angry, you ...

    ❏ Went and got it, complained to them and to the boss, and talked about it all day.

    ❏ Asked them politely and calmly if they were done with your stapler and brought it back to your desk when they were.

- You were late for the first time and your boss complained to you about that. Even though you were very upset and embarrassed, you ...

    ❏ Said calmly and respectfully, "I won't let it happen again."

    ❏ Complained that work starts too early, no one gets anything done before 10:00 a.m. anyway, and looked grumpy all day at work.

- A person you think is attractive at work is always very kind to you and smiles at you a lot. You feel strongly that this person wants to date you and you think you are in love. This person went to lunch with others and didn't invite you and you feel very hurt and angry. You ...

    ❏ Refuse to talk to them and complain to others about this person "cheating on you" all day.

    ❏ Continue to be calm and positive when you see this person at work.

- You just mopped the floor and someone walked on it with their dirty shoes, even though there was a "wet floor" sign. You feel extremely frustrated. You ...

    ❏ Stay calm, don't complain, and go back and mop that area again.

    ❏ Yell at the person, point at the wet floor sign, shove your mop hard into the pail, and leave the area.

*It is **positive** to work to develop "middle ground" (or less intensity) with your feelings if you regularly experience intense negative feelings.* Ways to do this include:

1. Always look for innocent reasons and simple explanations for what people say and do **first**. Most problems "just happen" because of circumstances or because circumstances change, are accidents, or happen because people (including you!) are not perfect. Be forgiving and feel your negative intensity go down.

2. Always remember that as a person on the autism spectrum, you may be challenged with "reading" the body language and meanings of others. Go slowly; think cautiously and with less intensity to give time for you to understand things fully.

Consider these situations and write what you can think to yourself and do to have less intense feelings.

You did not work fast enough, and you have to stay late to finish your work. Instead of being angry and feeling that the boss is always picking on you, say and think:

_____

_____

_____

_____

_____

You could not get your computer at work to log in again today and you feel intensely frustrated. Instead of thinking that "they just buy junk computers around here and nobody helps me," say and think:

_____

_____

_____

_____

_____

*It is **positive** to work to develop "middle ground" (or less intensity) with your opinions if you regularly experience intense opinions.* Ways to do this include:

1. Remember that everyone has their own opinions that are likely to be different than yours and that this is okay.

2. People, including you, may change their opinions over time, so you should be flexible and open to new ideas at all times.

3. Intense opinions are better not shared in the workplace, but if you do share an opinion, it is important to be tactful (see the "Word Choices" section of this book) to show respect for others, especially in the workplace.

On the lines below, state something that you feel very strongly is "right." Then check the boxes after it that move you toward middle ground and less intensity.

_____

_____

_____

But ...

❑ Other people may have a different opinion, and that is okay.

❑ I might change my opinion in time, so I will be flexible and open to new ideas.

❑ I will avoid stating my intense opinions at work, but if I do I will be tactful, respectful, and kind.

On the lines below, state something that you feel very strongly is "wrong." Then check the boxes after it that move you toward middle ground and less intensity.

_____

_____

_____

But ...

❑ Other people may have a different opinion, and that is okay.

❑ I might change my opinion in time, so I will be flexible and open to new ideas.

❑ I will avoid stating my intense opinions at work, but if I do I will be tactful, respectful, and kind.

*It is **positive** to do things that you don't prefer to do (while maintaining your positivity!) when you are asked to do them in the workplace.* You may intensely dislike certain jobs, or you may be intensely frustrated that you must work at all because it is preventing you from staying home and doing something you are passionately interested in doing (e.g., playing video games). You may feel intensely uncomfortable with the expectations of work, or intensely anxious about doing the work, interacting with others, or following the rules at work. Say each of the following things to yourself and mark the ones that you feel may help you the most to think about when you are asked to do what you do not like to do. Write in your own reason under "other" if you think of something you can say to yourself to help you out when you don't like something work-related. Then, think about the ones you picked every time you must do something you do not want to do related to work.

❑ People who have jobs also have income, independence, and relationships. I want and need those things.

❑ Someone has to do it.

❑ It is common to not like all aspects of one's job; it's the same for everyone else.

❑ I am being asked to do this work because my boss thinks I am capable.

❑ I am getting paid to do this work.

❑ If the work were easy, or if people volunteered to do it, they would not pay me to do it!

❑ I have to do it anyway, so I might as well do it with positivity and get credit for that.

❑ I might advance in my work to a different job if I cooperate with the work I am given now.

❑ I might learn something I can use later.

❑ I might develop friendships.

❑ I will be respected and have a good reputation.

❑ Other: _____

_____

_____

*It is **positive** to stop doing things that you prefer to do when it's time to work (while maintaining your positivity!).* Many individuals with ASD have intense interests or things they like to do. When you are at work you usually are not able to do those things; if you are allowed to do them during your break or at lunch time, you have to stop doing them when it is time to work again. Say each of the following things to yourself, and mark the ones that you feel may help you the most to think about when you are asked to stop doing what you prefer to do in order to go to work or when you go back to work after lunch or a break. Write in your own reason under "other" if you think of something else you can say to yourself that might help. Then, think about the ones you picked every time you must stop doing what you prefer to be doing and go to work.

❑ People who have jobs also have income, independence, and relationships. To get and keep a job I cannot do what I want during work time.

❑ I can't focus on work if I am focused on my favorite activity, and they are paying me to focus on work.

❑ Everyone at work is not doing their preferred activities; it's the same for everyone else.

❑ I am blending in with the my co-workers when I am doing the work activities and not doing my preferred activities.

❑ I am getting paid to do this work.

❑ If I were doing my favorite activity all day, they would not pay me.

❑ I have to stop my favorite activity to do work anyway, so I might as well do it on time and with positivity and get credit for that.

❑ I might advance in my work and earn more pay later if I cooperate with the work I am given now.

❑ I will be respected and have a good reputation.

❑ Other: _____

_____

_____

*It is **positive** to have alternative choices or acceptable options lined up in your mind, even if you have an intense desire or "first choice" that you want.* It is sometimes difficult to develop and accept alternatives when we have intense preferences. But since we so often don't get our first choice (and sometimes not even our second or third choices!) in the workplace, it is positive to be flexible! One way to help you be flexible is to consider second, third, or fourth choices.

Write something that you want very much (your "first choice") on the lines below.

_____

_____

_____

Now write down second, third, and fourth choice options that you would accept instead of your first choice, if you were unable to have your first choice.

Second choice:

_____

_____

Third choice:

_____

_____

Fourth choice:

_____

_____

* If you regularly practice coming up with alternatives to your "first choice" in this way, you will increase your flexibility in the workplace and in life, and that is positive!

It is **positive** *to tolerate being uncomfortable sometimes, so that you can grow emotionally, socially, and communicatively.* You need to bravely face and even embrace your discomfort as you work through your challenges in this book, because that is how you become more comfortable, more skilled, more positive, and more employable!

Choose a positive step that makes you uncomfortable, and do it. It can be a step from this book or some other positive step that makes you uncomfortable. Perhaps it is something that a parent or other trusted person has asked you to try to do, but you resisted because you were uncomfortable. After you do it, please write a reflection about it below.

What positive step makes me uncomfortable?

_____

_____

_____

What I did to practice it:

_____

_____

_____

What happened? (How I felt after doing it, how it changed me, etc.):

_____

_____

_____

What do I need to do in the future so that I can continue to grow and become more comfortable with this step or other steps?

_____

_____

_____

Lisa Tew is a speech-language pathologist who has worked with individuals on the autism spectrum from preschool through young adulthood for over thirty years in a variety of settings. In recent years, Lisa has worked with middle and high school students on the autism spectrum in the public school setting while also serving as transition coordinator, helping young people with disabilities transition to post-secondary education and employment. Additionally, Lisa works outside of the school setting with parents and young adults on the autism spectrum, in coordination with vocational services, to help develop the social communication soft skills needed for independence and employment. Lisa co-authored *Autism and Employment: Raising Your Child With Foundational Skills For The Future* (Future Horizons, 2018). You will find Lisa's blogs and Q&A responses on a variety of topics related to employment, social communication/soft skills, and independence at the Independent Futures With Autism website, IFAutism.com.